# RIDING SIDE-SADDLE

In memory of Sue Brenton, dear friend and tireless worker for side-saddle, who lost her battle with cancer just as I finished writing this book.

# Riding Side-saddle

## Janet W. Macdonald

J.A. Allen

London

British Library Cataloguing-in-Publication Data. A catalogue record for this book is available from the British Library.

ISBN 0.85131.621.2

Published in Great Britain in 1995 by
J.A. Allen & Company Limited
1 Lower Grosvenor Place, Buckingham Palace Road
London, SW1W 0EL

Typeset by Setrite Typesetters Ltd, Hong Kong
Printed by Dah Hua Printing Press Co. Ltd., Hong Kong

Illustrations by Maggie Raynor
Designed by Nancy Lawrence

Please note that I have referred throughout this book to riders as 'she' and horses as 'he'. This is in the interests of clarity, not for any sexist motive!

# Contents

# — Contents —

# List of Illustrations

# 1

# Learning a New Skill

Whether you are a complete beginner to riding or just want to add side-saddle to your existing riding skills, there are some basic principles of learning any physical skill which you should know, as this knowledge will make the learning process easier.

## Choosing a Teacher

Whilst you could, at a pinch, teach yourself to ride side-saddle, you are unlikely to teach yourself to do it well. There are several aspects of this which, as for any new physical skill, need a skilled observer to ensure that the newcomer does not fall into bad habits; and it does need a *skilled* observer. Anyone can stand behind you and tell you that you are not sitting straight, but it takes someone who knows what they are doing to tell you why and how to correct your posture.

So the first task is to find a good teacher who you can get on with. Both the Side-Saddle Association and the International Side-Saddle Organisation will send you a list of teachers in your area, but they cannot tell you whether these teachers will suit you. The only way to find this out is to go and see the teacher in action.

What you need in order to learn any new skill, whether it be side-saddle, tennis or knitting, is an instructor who can communicate with you. Far too many riding instructors lack this essential skill, assuming that the ability to ride well is all that is needed, and that shouting at their pupils will eventually get the message across. That might work if the pupil shares the

1

teacher's speech patterns and general inclinations, but if you are a person who likes detailed analytical explanations of why and how things happen, you will not learn anything from a teacher who just repeats the same phrase over and over, like a parrot. The best teachers are those who have a wide vocabulary and are prepared to reword instructions and explanations so that you can absorb them easily.

## The Processes of Learning

It will also help you to know at least the basics of how the brain works when you are learning new skills. There are two areas of interest here — technical and practical. The two technical concepts you should be aware of are kinaesthetics and proprioception.

Kinaesthetic memory is the brain's ability to take over sequences of action so that they can be repeated without conscious thought, and also its ability to remember the 'feel' of such sequences.

Proprioception is the human innate spatial awareness of the body and its component parts in relation to each other — the facility that allows you to shut your eyes and still be able to put a finger on the end of your nose. For the horse rider, it is what allows you to apply your leg in exactly the same place each time, and what allows you to feel trouble brewing underneath you when dragons threaten on a windy day.

Kinaesthetic memory is rather like an automatic pilot, in that it seeks to achieve an optimum feel for every situation (sometimes referred to as the 'resting state' principle). As a newcomer to side-saddle, it is going to cause you a little trouble, because it tells you things are wrong when they are just different, and this is why you need that knowledgeable person to reassure you about your position. Most riders adapt to accepting the new feel during the first lesson, but others take a bit longer. Oddly enough, it is the more experienced stride riders who tend to adapt quickly, although you would expect them to be more 'fixed' in their body feelings. This is probably because the experienced rider is more likely to ride a variety of horses, and is thus used to adapting to the slightly different feel of each horse.

Every rider will remember learning to rise to the trot. You bump and bounce, while the instructor calls 'Up down, up down, one two, one two', thinking you will never get it, then at last you catch the rhythm for a few strides, lose it and find it again, and then never have to think about it again. When your horse trots, you just think 'rise' and do it automatically. Your kinaesthetic memory scurries through your brain's data banks to find the instructions to tighten and relax muscles, read messages about the horse's speed and impulsion, and adjust your body accordingly.

Your brain will do all of this for you, but you can help it by not giving it too much new data to process at once. This is where the practical side of learning comes in. You will soon work out how much you can do at a time before you begin to suffer from 'information overload', but you may not realise that you will learn much faster if you break sessions into smaller chunks than the usual solid hour. Given that most teachers usually operate on an hourly basis, this may seem uneconomic, but in fact you will progress more quickly if you ride for two lots of twenty minutes with a twenty-minute break than if you ride for the solid hour.

This is partly to do with the 'concentration curve' and partly because the break seems to allow the brain to sort out what it has already learnt to apply it during the second session. For this reason, it is preferable to rest quietly during the break. It will also allow you to relax if you have any tendency to 'tizz up' during lessons.

One of the interesting things about riding, or any other skill, is the way little bits add up to a cohesive whole. It is rather like climbing a mountain that consists of a series of cliffs and plateaus. When you learn something, you climb a cliff, and then you cross the plateau as you consolidate that new knowledge into your existing knowledge.

When you start, the cliffs are small and the plateaus long, and it takes a long time to achieve any altitude. But as you progress, the cliffs get higher and the plateaus shorter — more like a series of steps — until the time comes when there are no more steps, just a steady, gentle slope to the top.

In the early stages, the cliffs are more likely to be related to equipment and clothing — little things like discovering that long boots are better than short ones, and leather better than rubber. For the side-saddle rider, it is often the revelation of how much difference a properly fitted saddle makes, or the discovery that the secure seat given by the saddle leads to a true independent seat which improves the functioning of the whole body — to such an extent that the mere process of learning to ride side-saddle also improves one's ability astride.

## Balance

It is necessary to adjust one's basic balance concepts to the fact that one no longer has a leg on either side of the horse. Few people realise that one of the things that helps hold you on a horse astride is the weight of your legs beneath you. On a side-saddle your legs are in front, but they are still lower than the rest of you and you can use them as a counter balance to the weight of the rest of your body.

Any side-saddle rider who has good balance should be capable of standing on the ground on her left foot with her right leg in her riding position and holding that stance for several minutes without over-balancing. It is actually worth practising this as it will help you achieve the correct seat and upper body position. Without a horse underneath you, you cannot remain upright if you lean or twist your torso!

## The Ideal Horse

The final consideration for the newcomer to side-saddle is whether the horse will be suitable. There is a (very small) school of thought that says horses have to be specially trained to carry a side-saddle, but in the author's not inconsiderable experience it is not necessary to do anything more than put the saddle on, climb on board and ride. The occasional horse is surprised by the balance strap, and for this reason it is wise to tighten that strap gently and then turn the horse through a few right-handed circles to let him feel the strap on his side before mounting.

The idea of special training is a hang-over from Victorian times when it was considered that a ladies' horse should not trot at all, and only canter on the right lead. When you wanted to go round a left-handed turn, you came down to walk, walked round the corner, then cantered again. In addition, the average horse in those days tended to have very rough manners, and most ladies only rode very gently round the countryside with a male escort, or in the park at the fashionable hour. A horse which was to be ridden by a lady had to be schooled to the stage where it was safe for these gentle pursuits and what we would consider to be a very novice rider. It wasn't until the 1870s, when the Empress of Austria made hunting an acceptable activity for ladies, that women learnt to gallop and jump and generally handle high-couraged horses.

As far as your own horse is concerned, all that is needed is conformation that gives a comfortable ride and allows the saddle to remain in place, and sufficient schooling to give you a safe and pleasurable ride. There are two aspects of conformation which are relevant.

A good wither is needed to hold the saddle in place, so any tendency towards loaded shoulders or excess weight which rounds the wither is not desirable. Some Arabians are rather round in the shoulder, and this, with a short back, may make them unsuitable for side-saddle. The other consideration is a good shoulder, as poor shoulders, which are often accompanied by a tendency to pick the knees up, give an uncomfortable jolting ride.

The notion of what constitutes 'sufficient schooling' is a subjective one, but a well-mannered, well-balanced horse will be a pleasure to ride in either saddle and an obnoxious animal will need schooling whether he is to be ridden side or stride. The important thing for a side-saddle horse is that he should be sufficiently well balanced to remain on his feet round left-handed corners, and that he should not evade the bit by hollowing his back and neck. Showing enthusiasts will, of course, require a lot more, but these are the essentials.

# 2

# Saddles

A good saddle, made of the best leather, and properly maintained, will last for decades. Unfortunately, so will a bad saddle, if it was made of good materials and lovingly maintained, and this has created a problem for the unsuspecting side-saddle buyer.

The side-saddle as we know it today was developed between ·the two world wars. Before the first war, although they had evolved from the dipped seats of the previous century, side-saddles had narrow pommels, with parallel sides, and they almost all had plain leather seats. During the 1930s, the pommel developed into a wide-based triangle, and both pommel and seat were usually covered with doeskin. (Some riders still prefer a leather seat, but these do tend to be slippery.)

Because the old-fashioned saddles were superbly made, many of them are still in a usable condition but they are not suitable for beginners. Alas, although some of their trading names still exist, the skilled manufacturers from between the wars have now all disappeared. There have been some modern attempts to make new side-saddles, but in general these have not been acceptable.

The problem is that a side-saddle is asymmetrical. It is not just a cross-saddle with pommels and a levelled seat; you cannot build a proper side-saddle on a cross-saddle tree. This does not mean that people don't try to do this, so suspect any brand new saddle with a high cantle and equal lengthed tree points.

## Level Seat

Another serious problem with these saddles is the manufacturer's interpretation of the term 'level seat'. Although it is often stated that the seat on a good side-saddle is absolutely level, this is not strictly true. At a glance, the seat on one of the classic makes of side-saddle (Owen, Mayhew, Whippy, Champion & Wilton) does appear to be level, but when you look more closely you can see that it has been very carefully shaped not only to accommodate the shape of the female thighs and seat, but also to place the rider's weight precisely where it should be.

From front to back there is a dip of about 1 inch (25 mm) and the front, by the pommels, is slightly higher than the back. This accommodates the buttocks and the taper of thigh muscle from buttock to knee. From side to side the wide part of the seat and the very back of the seat are scooped out on the right to ensure that most of the rider's body weight is placed on her right seatbone where it should be. This shaping is built into the saddle from the tree up and it is inherent in the tree itself. The positioning and comfort it gives the rider cannot be achieved by extra padding in the seat or by extra padding in the nearside panel.

Without this 'levelness' of seat, it is impossible to sit straight and face the front without contorting the spine. The Victorian dip-seated saddles positioned the rider facing her horse's left shoulder and she then had to twist her torso to face the front. It is hardly surprising that it was thought that riding side-saddle induced curvature of the spine. A later development, in the 1880s, was a stepped seat with the pommels very close together. This made it easier to lean back over fences as was the fashion, but it doesn't allow you to adopt the modern, more forward seat.

For that, the seat must be 'level' as above, and it must be horizontal. If it is not, you will never be able to sit properly, for the saddle will tip you over. This will create muscle strains which will impede your body control and it will probably make the saddle pinch your horse.

The classic example of this is the saddle which tilts to the

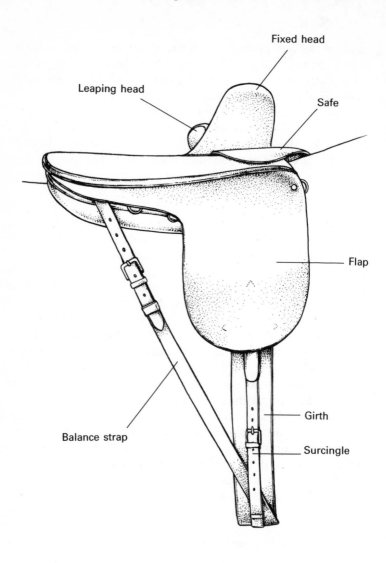

Figure 1a  Parts of the side-saddle (offside)

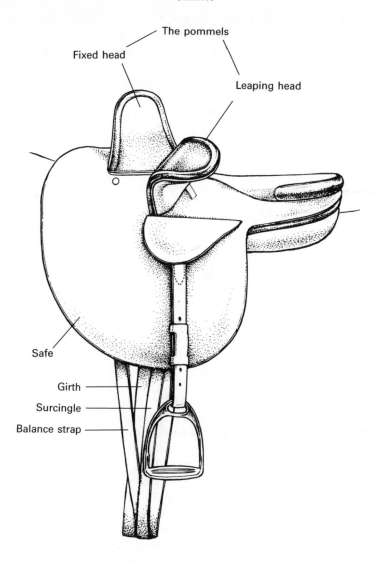

The pommels

Fixed head

Leaping head

Safe

Girth

Surcingle

Balance strap

Figure 1b Parts of the side-saddle (nearside)

left at the back. It makes your left hip drop, your left side swings back, and your horse moves crab-wise because he is carrying his quarters in away from your weight. In this situation, although some temporary remedial action can be taken with a foam pad, the only permanent solution is to get the saddle properly fitted to the horse.

This is not a job which any saddler can do, so you need to call on a specialist side-saddler. They will charge a journey fee as well as the fitting fee, but this is a small price to pay for the superb feel of a saddle which actually fits your horse. (Take the opportunity to have your cross saddle done at the same time.)

## Fitting to the Horse

Done properly, the saddle will be fitted to the horse, not just re-stuffed as is normally done with cross saddles. The final adjustments need the rider to sit on the saddle, so the saddler must have both on hand while he works. He does not remove the panel, but unpicks a few stitches at the edge of the lining and applies (or removes) stuffing through the gap. When he has it more or less as he thinks it should be, he will put it on the horse and ask you to sit on it. Then he will make any last adjustments before resewing the lining. This procedure will take about an hour.

The art in fitting a side-saddle lies in placing you exactly where you ought to be. To an inexperienced eye, a properly fitted saddle on the horse without its rider looks as though it has been over-stuffed on the nearside, because it will actually tilt down to the offside all along. Once you are on top, the weight of both of your legs on the nearside will level it and you will be sitting on a level surface.

The stuffing should be organised so that your weight is borne on the inner two-thirds of the offside of the saddle and the outer third of the nearside. At the front, under the points of the tree, there should be most stuffing under the bottom on the nearside point, tapering to nothing at the top; and on the offside (where the point is much shorter) there should be most stuffing at the top, tapering to nothing at the bottom. It is more likely to be incorrect stuffing on the front offside which causes the saddle to tip backwards to the left, than insufficient or compressed stuffing on that back corner.

It should go without saying that neither at the front nor at the back should the saddle touch the horse's spine. If someone tells you that this is happening with your saddle you should dismount immediately and not use the saddle again until it has been properly fitted, as otherwise you could do permanent damage to your horse.

It is comparatively easy to make a side-saddle fit a horse, assuming that the saddle has a normal panel and the horse has a normal back and wither. For the horse with no wither, or loaded shoulders, or just too much fat, the answer could be a Wykeham pad. This is a detachable thick felt pad which serves instead of a conventional panel. They were invented for hunting ladies who had several horses − one saddle top fitted the rider, and she had a different pad to fit each horse. You cannot adjust the stuffing, for there is none, but they are much more accommodating to a wide-backed horse.

## Choosing a Saddle to Fit You

It is not so easy to adjust a saddle to fit the rider without major expense. A certain amount can be done to alter the leaping-head, since it is screwed on to the saddle and has an iron bar inside the cover. This cover can be slipped off and minor alterations made to the curvature of the bar by a blacksmith, but you cannot do too much or the leather of that pommel will not lie flat and may tear. You could have a new cover made, but this will be expensive.

You cannot alter the shape or location of the fixed-head, and it is the fixed-head which determines whether the saddle fits you. The point at issue here is the size and shape of your right thigh and also your hips and buttocks. The first consideration is the length. Side-saddles are described by their length, which is measured from the back of the cut-out by the fixed-head to the back of the seat. This coincides with the length of the rider's thigh − the average 5 ft 4 ins rider will have a 16 inch thigh.

When you buy a saddle for yourself, you should seek the proper length, but for lessons it does not matter too much if

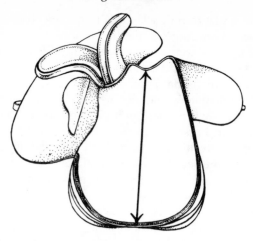

Figure 1c Side-saddles are measured across the centre of the seat. This corresponds to the length of the rider's thigh

the saddle is too long for you. What will not do is a saddle that is too short, as this will put all your weight on the very back of the saddle, which will then be pressed down onto the horse's back.

As far as width is concerned, there should not be any bits of you overlapping the seat, or you will be most uncomfortable. Ideally, the edge of your jacket and apron should just touch the saddle.

The second, and more important consideration when choosing your saddle, assuming that the length, width and leaping-head are acceptable, is the position of the fixed-head on the top of the saddle. Keeping in mind that your right femur should be parallel to the horse's spine, and that your right knee should be snug against the fixed-head, it follows that the fixed-head should be positioned and stuffed to allow both these essentials. But different ladies have different amounts of flesh and muscle on their thighs, and your fixed-head should be in the proper place for your thigh.

In the days when your side-saddle was made for you, the saddler allowed for this difference; larger thighed ladies had a fixed-head well to the left, or sparsely stuffed, while smaller thighed ladies had a fixed head well to the right or with lots of stuffing. Put a large lady on a small lady's saddle and her femur will angle to the right and there is nothing you can do to correct it. Put a small lady on a large lady's saddle and her femur will angle to the left, either making her sit crooked or inviting her to sit too far to the left, 'alongside' her horse. Not only does this look dreadful, it is likely to bring the horse down on left-handed bends. In the latter case, if the discrepancy is not too great, you can alleviate the problem with a 'queen' (a fitted addition which straps on) or by wrapping the fixed-head with a bandage.

Leaping-heads were also made for the rider's thigh, and the curvature on a small lady's saddle will be too tight for the large lady and vice versa.

If you find a saddle which is a perfect fit for you, but which has a slippery leather seat, don't despair. You can wear suede-seated breeches, put gymnast's resin on the seat, or – and here you have to be *very* careful – rough the seat with a knife or a metal suede brush. Or, of course, you can have a new top put on, but this is an expensive undertaking.

The other major consideration when buying a side-saddle is that it must have a proper safety stirrup. Older saddles had either a 'D' ring or roller bar on the saddle, with an ordinary stirrup leather and iron, but these are very dangerous as they will not come off the saddle if you do have a fall. Modern saddles have a quick-release fitting at the top of the stirrup leather, which allows the whole stirrup to come off the saddle.

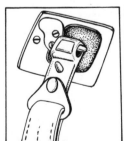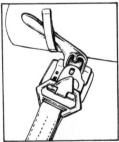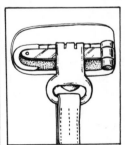

Figure 2a  Modern safety stirrup fittings (from left to right: Owen, Champion & Wilton, Mayhew)

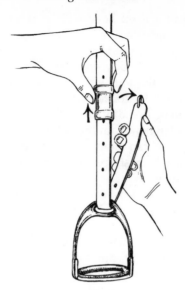

Figure 2b Adjusting stirrup length

These devices vary according to the make of the saddle, and they are not interchangeable. With the exception of the Mayhew type, where the tongue-flap must be on the inside, they cannot be put on incorrectly.

Old-fashioned stirrup-irons come in many forms, all patented to break open in one way or another. This was meant to prevent the rider's foot getting trapped if she fell, but they weren't very satisfactory and are often very small. Modern irons look very much like cross-saddle irons, except that they have an extra large eye to allow the adjusting hook through.

Stirrup length is most easily adjusted from the ground, but if someone else does it for you, warn them to ensure that their thumb is on the side of the leather when they slip the hook cover up. Otherwise, if the cover is stiff and suddenly gives, it is easy to run the hook into the ball of the thumb.

Once the cover is raised, just unhook the leather and re-hook it in the correct place before sliding the cover back down. If the cover stretches it is wise to have it replaced straight away as otherwise the hook could damage your boot.

## Girths and Balance Straps

There is nothing special about girths for side-saddles, although they may need to be a little longer than for a cross-saddle. Some people like a lampwick girth for showing, but for everyday use, leather is best. Fabric girths can distort with the weight of the saddle on the shoulders, and will then wrinkle and rub, while string girths tend to stretch over time.

If the saddle fits the horse properly, there is no need for the girth to be any tighter than usual. If there is a tab-strap on the off-side, use it, as this helps to keep the front of the saddle down.

With the exception of some early saddles made by Champion & Wilton, which had a buckle on the nearside tree-point and thus needed a special balance strap, most saddles have a separate tab-strap for the balance strap. Some of these are angled backwards, but this angle should be very slight or it will invite the balance strap to slip backwards. The balance strap should stay with the girth as it passes under the horse and should be fastened tightly enough to keep the back of the saddle still. (This is particularly important when you start learning to ride side-saddle, as if you bump about before you get your balance, you could give your horse a sore back.)

The balance strap need not be done up so tightly as to inconvenience the horse. Its purpose is to stop the back of the saddle moving about, not to weld the saddle on. On the other hand, it should not be so loose that it can slip backwards, as this can make a sensitive horse buck.

Some show people like a small balance strap sewn on to the offside of the girth, but this arrangement does require perfect saddle fitting and a rider who can sit perfectly still, so it is best left to experienced riders.

Where the saddle has a separate flap-strap, this need only be tight enough to hold the flap down. Martin & Martin saddles have a metal spring instead of a strap.

## Putting the Saddle On

When you put your saddle on for the first time, be sure there

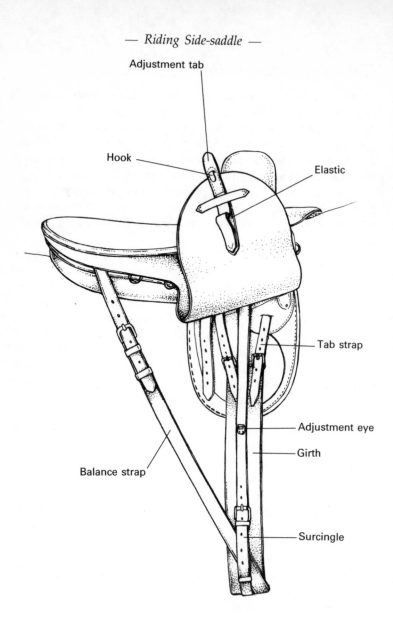

Adjustment tab

Hook

Elastic

Tab strap

Adjustment eye

Girth

Balance strap

Surcingle

Figure 3a  Correct fitting of girth and balance strap (offside)

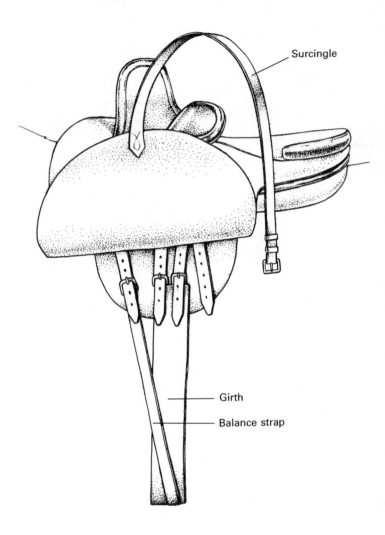

Figure 3b Correct fitting of girth and balance strap (nearside)

Figure 4a Two alternative ways to carry a side-saddle

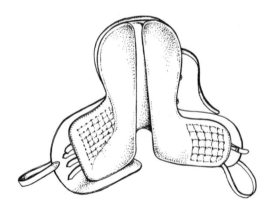

Figure 4b The correct way to put a side-saddle down

is someone there who can check it for you. Quite apart from all the unfamiliar straps, it is easy to put the saddle on too far forward, and it then slopes backwards or pinches the horse's shoulders.

Don't put the saddle on in the stable or a horse box, as the pommels could catch on the door as you lead your horse out. See figures 4a and 4b for how to carry the saddle and how to lay it down. And don't ever be tempted to hang the stirrup iron over the pommels, as this damages the leather.

Use ordinary saddle soap to clean the pigskin parts of your saddle. For the doeskin, you will need a suede brush or a very sharp knife. The knife is used at right angles to the surface, and you scrape *very* carefully. If the doeskin gets really foul, a little washing-up liquid in warm water should shift it. Cleaning the underside is less easy. In hot countries the lining may be leather, but otherwise it will be serge, overlined with linen. If it is damp, it must be allowed to dry before scraping the sweat off with a blunt knife. You will occasionally want to scrub it with washing-up liquid (nothing stronger which could affect the horse's skin) and a nail brush, but do not use too much water and soak the stuffing. For lessons or hacking, you might like to use a saddle-cloth, but you cannot do so in competitions.

There are a few offside saddles around. Most of these were made for disabled riders who could not ride on the nearside, and they tend to have other peculiarities beside the pommel position. Unless you have a disability which prevents you from riding on the nearside, don't be tempted to buy one of these saddles, as you will need a specially made apron, and you will have difficulty selling the saddle if you decide you don't want it.

All of the above comments refer mainly to 'English' side-saddles, but there are also Western or Stock side-saddles, although these are mostly quite old and vary considerably. They are rigged like any other stock saddle and few have balance straps, although some do have holsters for lady-like guns! The problem with most of them is that they do not have level seats and thus do not allow the rider to face the front comfortably.

# 3

# Mounting and Dismounting

The best way to get up onto a side-saddle is with a leg-up. The next best way is from a tall mounting block. The worst way, and one to be avoided whenever possible, is to mount from the ground with no one to help you. Even with someone on the offside holding the saddle, you will inevitably shift the saddle as you pull yourself up, and you will never get it back into the proper place without dismounting. You are then hindering yourself by trying to ride on an unlevel saddle and also risk scalding your horse's back in the process.

If circumstances force you to mount from the ground alone, try to find some way of getting yourself higher than your horse's feet. This could be by using a tree stump, a curb-stone, or even sloping ground. Make it easier by letting the stirrup down a few holes, and don't try to pull yourself up by the leaping-head. Finally, mount astride and then swing your right leg over, rather than try the dangerous manoeuvre of bringing your right foot between your left leg and the saddle.

## The Classic Method

The classic method of mounting requires a light rider and a strong legger-up, preferably male. This does not mean that a female can't give you this sort of leg-up, but few women have the strength to give you the slow controlled lift you need. You will need considerable practice to achieve the beautiful unbroken movement of stepping from the ground onto your assistant's hand and thence straight into your riding position,

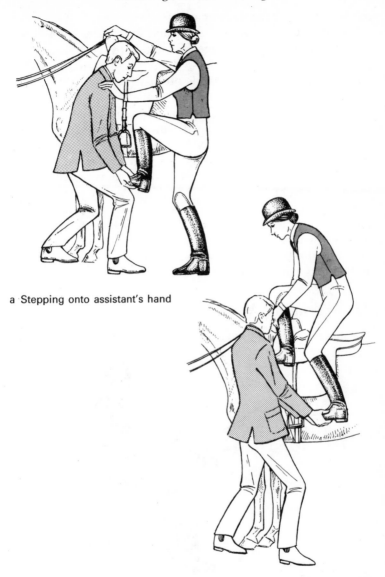

a Stepping onto assistant's hand

b Springing up and leaning to the right

Figure 5 Mounting by the classic method

but it is worth it for the elegant effect.

You also need a horse who will stand still, or another assistant to hold the horse. The legger-up stands by your horse's left shoulder, facing the quarters, with his right foot forward, knees bent and cups his hands on his right knee. You stand, facing front, with your right hand on the saddle (as far over to the offside as you can reach) your left hand on his shoulder, and your left foot in his cupped hands. On the agreed signal, you step onto your left foot as though climbing upstairs, spring up off your right foot and straighten your left leg. At the same time, he straightens his legs and lifts his hands, and then you bring your right knee forward and up. When you are high enough to clear the pommels, lean your body to the right, shift your hips to the right, and bend your left knee to bring your seat down onto the saddle with your right leg in position round the fixed head. Your assistant then offers you the stirrup and adjusts your apron.

## An Alternative Method

The next method, which allows you to take a leg-up from

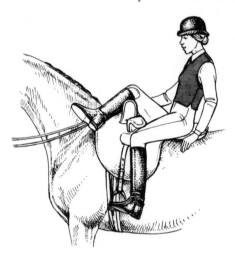

Figure 6 After arriving on the saddle with both legs on the nearside, adjust position by bringing the right leg over the pommel

anyone, is to take an ordinary leg-up to land with both legs on the nearside of the saddle. For this, you stand facing front and turn in mid-air to land with your buttocks on the seat and your legs facing left, both behind the pommels. Then all you need do is swing your right leg over the pommels before settling yourself in your final position. (It is a good idea to wait for your assistant to step back before you swing your right leg, as otherwise you might kick him in the teeth!) This method is not advisable for beginners, as it involves a certain amount of wriggling about to get yourself organised.

## *Mounting Astride for Beginners*

Beginners should always mount astride to ensure they are absolutely central before bringing the right leg over. Whether or not you have a mounting block available, you will need at least one assistant the first few times you mount. One of them is going to stand behind you to check that you are central, and

Figure 7 An ordinary leg-up, but rider must stand back further than usual to avoid the pommels

23

the other is going to hold your horse while you sort yourself out. Even if your horse does stand rock still, you will need both hands to do other things besides holding the reins.

When you prepare to mount, remember that you are going to be sitting further back than you do astride, and that the pommels occupy the place where you would usually sit. This means that you have to stand a bit behind the wither when you have a leg-up. Because you don't want to arrive in the saddle with an undignified scramble, be sure that your assistant knows what he is doing. It is surprising how many people do it badly, when the correct way is so easy.

You should stand on your right foot, keeping your right thigh parallel to the other and raise your left foot behind you until the knee joint is at a right angle. Lock that knee joint and keep your thighs parallel until you are in the air and ready to swing your right leg over the saddle. Your assistant stands a little behind and to your left, bends his knees (not his back), cups his left hand under your left knee and his right hand under your left ankle, ideally from the outside, not the inside. Then, on the agreed signal, you spring and he lifts and straightens his knees. He should do no more than lift straight up, not pull in any direction, as this will tip you over. He should not grip your ankle, nor try to lift it with his hip, as these actions will also unbalance you.

With an assistant who has not helped you before, it may be worth a few dummy runs to establish exactly what you mean by the signal, as you do not want to arrive on the saddle with a thump. Most people say 'one – two – three', but some mean 'three and up' while others think 'three' means up.

## Adjusting the Seat for Beginners

The first few times you get onto a side-saddle, you should sit astride while your assistant goes behind to make sure you are absolutely central. Assuming that your breeches seam is over your spine, all they have to do is line that seam up with the horse's spine. Once they are happy, they can help you put your left foot into the stirrup and adjust it if necessary. Now you can organise your right leg. Before you do anything else, place your right hand on the offside of the saddle where the balance strap starts, and then swing your right leg up and round the fixed head. Obviously it is easier to do this if your horse's head is down.

Then, with your left hand, check that you have a couple of fingers' clearance between your right knee and the front of the fixed-head. If there is much more, or much less, do not wriggle to adjust your leg, but bring it back to sit astride again before moving your seat back or forward as necessary. Then, once your assistant has checked that you are still central, you can bring the leg over again.

When you mount without anyone around to hold your horse, you hold your reins and whip in your left hand, just as you would astride. If you are wearing your habit, you turn the apron back over your left forearm and leave it there until you are settled in your riding position and ready to wrap it round your right leg and put the elastic over your foot.

Figure 8 Dismounting

## *Dismounting*

To dismount, put reins and whip in your right hand. (This allows you to keep control of your horse.) Unfasten the foot elastic of your apron and turn it back over your left arm, then take your foot out of the stirrup. Swivel your seat until you face the nearside and swing your right leg over the pommels so both legs are on the nearside. Put your right hand, still holding reins and whip, on top of the fixed head.

Next, to resist the temptation to lean on the leaping head and also to prevent your jacket catching on it (and removing the buttons!) put your left hand on your bottom jacket button. Half jump, half slide to the ground, turning to face front as you go and landing lightly on the balls of your feet with a slight 'knees bend' to prevent jarring yourself. Don't forget that the side-saddle effectively makes the horse a hand higher than usual.

Described like this it looks complicated, but of course it isn't. This is the most graceful way to dismount and also the safest as it leaves you in full command of your horse all the time.

# 4

# The Basic Position

## The Right Thigh

The whole art of riding side-saddle is dependent on the right leg. For this reason it is worth spending a lot of time getting it into the correct position before you move off, and, during your early lessons, stopping at regular intervals to check that it hasn't shifted.

A number of misleading phrases describing the position and weight-carrying importance of the right leg have evolved over the years, and it is worth discussing these so that you are clear about what is desirable and what happens if you get it wrong. The first of these phrases is 'the right thigh should be parallel to the horse's spine'. The problem with this is that thighs are not parallelograms, but elongated triangles, and the phrase doesn't say which part of the thigh it means. If you think about it, you realise that it can't mean the outer edge of the thigh, for that would put all of the rider's hips and torso on the left side of the horse. Nor can it mean the thigh bone, for that would have almost the same effect.

The closest is the inner edge, for at least this would allow your hips to sit centrally over the spine. But it still isn't correct, because unless you have a very fat knee, or a fixed head that is placed with its inner surface right in the middle of the saddle (which they aren't) to hold your leg so that the inner thigh is parallel to the horse's spine would leave a very large gap between knee and fixed head.

The truth of the matter is that your right thigh crosses your horse's spine at a gentle angle, closer to your knee than to your hips. This leads us to the next misconception — 'your weight should be carried at the point where your thigh crosses your horse's spine'. Given that this point is close to your knee, it is virtually impossible to put your weight over it unless you lift your behind from the saddle and lean well forward like a showjumper in mid flight. And this is where the idea comes from. When the forward seat became popular just after the second war, some hunting ladies thought it should apply to side-saddle as well 'and went to great trouble to have their saddles adapted to allow them to get well forward when jumping big fences. Unless you expect to spend a lot of time jumping seriously large fences, and only when you are doing that, you do not need to worry about it.

Some variations on this erroneous theme are 'your weight should be carried on the outside of your right thigh'; 'roll over onto the outside edge of your right thigh'; or 'imagine there is a tin-tack under your left hip'. These phrases have come about in the attempt to correct riders who allow their weight to drop back on their left hip, but they cause the rider who obeys them to develop a banana-like curve in her back.

The answer to the whole thing is that you have to adjust the muscles of your right thigh to put yourself in the correct position. Consider the inner surface of the human thigh. Because of the way the muscles are formed, men's thighs are flat on the inside, which makes it easier for them to sit astride a horse without their toes pointing out. Women's thighs are much rounder generally, and this is why so many of us have the 'penguin feet' problem when we ride. The solution to the problem astride is to pull your thigh muscles behind you manually so that the surface presented to the saddle is flat. The same applies to side-saddle — you need a flat thigh surface on the saddle and you achieve this with your right thigh by pulling the muscle to the inside rather than the outside.

All you have to do is to lift your right thigh a little, reach in under it with your left hand, and shift the muscle to the inside before putting the leg down. Not only does this put your leg in the correct position, it prevents your hips from rolling, makes the fixed head fit more snugly round your knee, and also makes it easier to keep your right calf against the saddle.

## *Weight Distribution* _____

Your weight should not be equally distributed on both seat
bones, but nor should it be mostly on the right seat bone, as is
often suggested, since this makes the hips tilt. Where it should
be is on the front edge of the left seatbone and on the centre
of the right seatbone, with the pelvis just fractionally tilted
forward. This should prevent the most common fault, that of
allowing the left hip to drop back.

## *The Left Leg* _____

The left leg should be in your normal riding position, with the
exception that you should not try to wrap it round the horse.
This will bring the knee off the saddle and out from under the
leaping head. You should be able to get the flat of your hand
between your leg and the leaping head, for its purpose is to
help in emergencies, not to keep you on the saddle all the
time. The foot should be everted, so that an observer on the
ground can just see the sole of your boot. The easiest way to

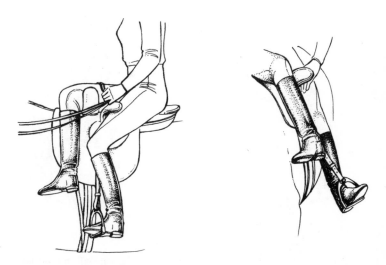

Figure 9 Correct position of legs, with room to slide the hand between the
left thigh and the leaping head

achieve this is to keep your lower leg firmly against the saddle while stretching your little toe up and out, as though you were drinking a cup of tea with your little finger cocked.

## The Right Foot

The right foot should also be turned out, by which I mean out from your centre, not out away from the horse. The outside of the right calf and foot should be pressed quite firmly against your horse's shoulder, with the toe down. If you turn your toe up, it will push your knee up off the saddle, and you shouldn't allow this to happen. Tell yourself to pull your knee down with your toes and all should be well.

This position of the right leg is known as 'purchase' and it is this that keeps you on the saddle, even when jumping. Beginners tend to assume that the side-saddle seat is dependent on a scissors grip with the legs on the pommels. It may help to apply such a grip in a dire emergency, but it is neither necessary nor desirable otherwise.

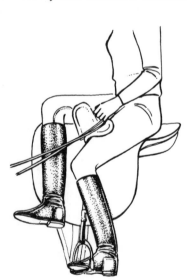

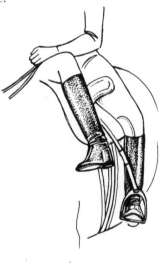

a  too far forward with left thigh jammed too close to leaping head

b  rider is crooked and left leg is turned out. In an emergency, the left leg will come out from under the leaping head

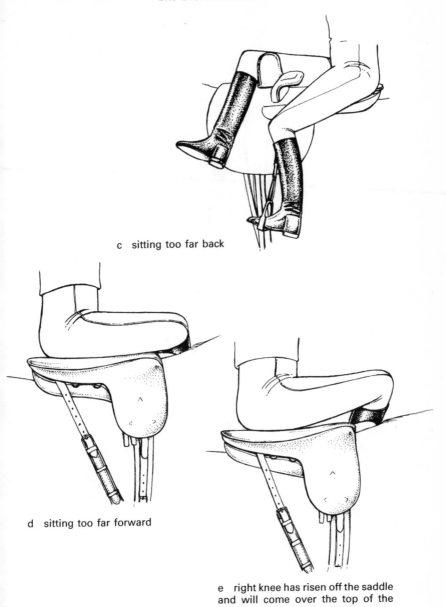

c  sitting too far back

d  sitting too far forward

e  right knee has risen off the saddle and will come over the top of the fixed head in an emergency

Figure 10 Incorrect position of legs

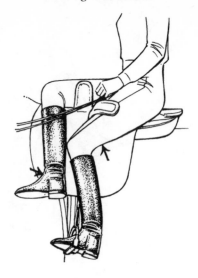

Figure 11 Applying the emergency grip

If you find that your right foot slides forwards, you may need to get some additional padding put under the safe of your saddle. Some saddles do not have any at all, and your horse may have less meat on his shoulders than the original wearer.

The final thing that helps to lock you on to the saddle is your right shoulder. The command 'Right shoulder back!' is too frequently used when the left hip has dropped back, but assuming that everything else is correct, tweaking your right shoulder back — and this does mean just the shoulder, nothing else — flexes the muscles across the front of your right hip and the top of your thigh and locks your right knee firmly on to the fixed head.

## Sitting Correctly

You should now be sitting with your spine perpendicular and immediately over your horse's spine, your hips and shoulders horizontal and square to the horse's spine. This assumes that your body is perfectly symmetrical. Many people are slightly asymmetrical, especially if they are strongly 'handed'. Most dominantly right-handed people have a right shoulder that slopes more than the left, and many right-handed women have a right breast that is slightly larger than the other. Skilled tailors have always been aware of this, and compensate by padding the right shoulder of the jacket. If you are built like this, and see yourself in a mirror and think you are crooked, get someone to look at you from behind and check your spine rather than try to hold your right shoulder up.

There is a simple way to check for yourself whether you are sitting straight and centrally. Make sure your horse is standing square, then sit with your head up and cast your eyes down. Project an imaginary line down your breastbone to just below

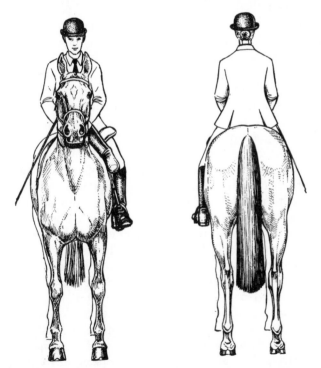

Figure 12 Correct position, with the rider sitting absolutely centrally

your navel, then turn the line through a right angle and send it out in front of you. If you are sitting straight, square, and with your spine over the horse's, your line will go over his wither, up the centre of his neck and between his ears. If it goes straight, but to one side, you are sitting straight but not centrally. If it goes off to one side of him at neck level but at an angle, you are sitting straight but you have twisted yourself to face left or right. If it goes up in the air as well as at an angle, you are leaning sideways. All you need do is adjust your position until that line goes up his neck and out between his ears.

One little tip is to make sure that whenever anyone on the ground talks to you, they stand on the offside to do so. This will encourage you to turn that way rather than turning to the left with the ever present danger of dropping your weight back to the left.

A common problem with newcomers to side-saddle is that they tend to slump. They may well do it astride, as well, but it looks much worse on a side-saddle. You should always strive to look elegant, and this is dependent on your being erect but relaxed. Teachers tend to tell you to 'Sit up straight', which is all right as long as you don't overdo it and make yourself rigid by hollowing your back and tucking in your chin.

Think instead of sitting tall and elegant; drawn up to your full height; having a bad smell under your nose; or, in the words of the yoga maxim, pushing your shoulders away from your ears. If it is just your shoulders that are at fault, try the old deportment teacher's trick of rolling your shoulders up, back and down. All of this is easier if your elbows are close to your sides by your waist. If you allow them to creep forward your upper body will tend to follow them.

Many riders, astride as well as aside, sit reasonably erect but look down all the time. It is not surprising, in a world that is increasingly visually oriented, that when you are concentrating on your body, you should be tempted to look down at it, but you must resist that temptation. Remember that bad smell under your nose, or think of yourself as a puppet hanging from a string through the centre of your head; or try the Guards trick of tilting your hat forward until you can't see in front of

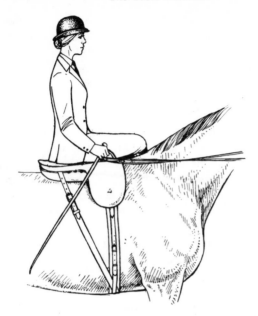

Figure 13a Correct position (offside)

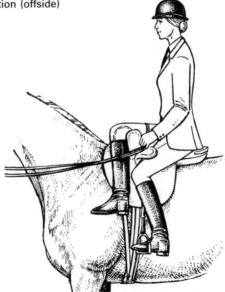

Figure 13b Correct position (nearside)

you unless your head is up. If you drive a car, maladjust the interior mirror upwards a little, so you have to raise your head to see in it, and you will soon lose the habit.

A good exercise to get you sitting properly is a variation on the 'right shoulder back' theme. Sit facing front and bring your right arm up in front of you. When it is straight and horizontal, rotate it until your palm is upwards. Now sweep the whole of your arm, your shoulders and your head to the right through 90 degrees, with your arm remaining at shoulder height. This causes your torso to pivot to the right as well, tightening up those muscles which lock the knee onto the fixed head. Then, without moving your torso or shoulders, drop the arm gently and finally turn your head back to the front.

Sit like that quietly for a moment, memorising the feel of the muscles in your torso and right leg. This is the feel you should have all the time you are on a side-saddle. When you are ready to relax, do so by 'dropping' the tension onto your right seatbone, but be careful not to lean to the right when you do this. You should now have your weight distributed just where it should be. Do this exercise every time you get on the saddle and at any time when you have paused for a rest.

## Importance of Balance

The purpose of all this is not just to make you look elegant, but to ensure that you are balanced and in full, fine, control of your body. If you are not able to control yourself, you will never be able to control your horse. No part of your body is independent of the rest, and whether you are astride or aside, imbalance creates major muscle tension in either your back or stomach muscles as they strive to hold the body upright.

Try this exercise to see the effects of these tensions. Sit on a stool, or better still, a 'Balans' chair (the Scandinavian back-care chairs where you half-kneel, half-sit). First, sit nicely balanced with your head directly above your shoulders and your shoulders directly above your hips. Raise your arms and move them around to feel how freely they move. Then adjust your sitting position to tuck your backside under you and lean back and move your arms around again. You will find a major tension in your stomach muscles, as they strive to hold you up, and you will also find you have very little free movement in your arms.

Adjust your sitting position again, to push your seat out behind you and lean forward. This time it will be your back muscles that are protesting and impeding your movement. Then try it with a lean to one side and you will find that both back and stomach muscles will now come into play, with a major restriction of free movement. Then try the whole set again, this time sitting on the edge of a table with your right thigh along the top and your right calf dangling over the edge. The seat position is different, but the muscle tensions and restrictions are exactly the same.

The best teachers will concentrate on getting your basic seat and balance correct before they fuss about refinements like your hands and feet. It is very important, when you learn a new physical skill, that you teach your kinaesthetic memory what is the 'correct' feel for each bit of your body, because once it is firmly in the memory, you can consign it to automatic pilot while you learn the next bit.

For this reason it is helpful to have someone to lead or lunge your horse at your first lesson, so you can concentrate on the feel instead of having to worry about guiding him. There are two schools of thought on lungeing side-saddle. The first considers it essential, while the other feels it gives an excessive bend and thus a false feeling. If you would feel happier on the lunge, choose a horse who is used to it and who neither swings his quarters out nor breaks the rhythm of his gaits.

## Hand Position

Whether or not you are guiding your horse during your early lessons, you should still hold your hands properly. This is something which often puzzles beginners, as they cannot work out where they should be. The answer to the puzzle is that your hands should be where your horse expects to find them, which means on the end of reins that are at a tension he is used to and which come to the bit at an angle he is used to.

Figure 14a Acceptable hand position with hands either side of the right thigh. This is the most commonly seen position today

This can be achieved despite the length of rein from mouth to hand being greater, so you should not try to carry your hands where they would be in relation to your horse astride. For the average British rider, this position is somewhere close to the withers, but on a side-saddle you cannot get your hands there at the correct angle without considerable contortion. Even if you ignore the angle, carrying your hands that far forward on a side-saddle means you would have to lean forward or straighten your arms, neither of which is desirable.

Since the side-saddle seat is both further back and higher up than astride, all you need to do is to allow the normal line of rein from horse's mouth to your hands to lengthen by about eight inches. This continues the line to a point where it meets your hands without destroying your posture. For American riders, whether riding saddle-, stock- or hunt-seat, the same principle applies.

The hands themselves should be as for astride — knuckles vertical and the wrists bent in a little; and they should be carried in one of the two classic positions. The first, with one hand either side of, and level with the right thigh, is the most suitable for beginners or novice horses. The second, for advanced riders and well-balanced and light horses, is with the hands in the lap, knuckles almost touching. In both situations your arms should hang straight down from your shoulders, close to your sides and with your forearms horizontal.

Figure 14b  The classic hand position with the hands in the lap; only suitable for a well-schooled, well-mannered horse

To help you resist the temptation to stick your elbows out, or to lean on your forearms, keep them just above rather than resting on your thigh. It is actually quite difficult to hold your elbows out unless your arms are rigid, so if you have a tendency to do this you may have a tension problem or you may have turned your hands over. The hand position known as the 'pram pusher' causes the bones in your forearm to cross over and lock, stiffens the wrist and pushes your elbows out. Quite apart from the stiffness, this position prevents your actually using the reins, as you can only do so by pulling your arms back with your elbow going back and out. This is not only very ugly, it does not allow enough pull in an emergency. (Nor does a pair of reins which is looped round the front of your knee.)

Think of holding a tray of coffee as well as the reins, or imagine you are carrying a little bird in each hand. If you turn your hands over, you will bang their heads together. Thinking of these little birds (or a dog's squeaky toy) is also useful if you have a tendency to grip the reins too tightly, as you wouldn't want to crush them to death.

Another temptation which you must avoid is to carry both hands on the right side of your right thigh, as this gives both direct and indirect rein aids at once.

There is an idea among some showing people that the right hand should be carried very low when riding side-saddle, to 'lengthen the horse's front'. Maybe it does, and for that reason it might be desirable when you first enter the ring in walk, but when it is carried to such an extreme that the right hand is held below the right hip, with a totally straight arm, it most certainly impedes the horse's freedom of movement. Even without such extremes, it comes under the heading of Ringcraft, and should not be used in normal riding, nor confused with the indirect rein of opposition.

(This use of the low right hand is sometimes thought to be the answer to horses who drift to the right, but since this is usually caused by the rider's weight dropping back to the left, it is preferable to correct that fault rather than try to compensate for it.)

With the exception of American riders on western side-saddles, who will naturally continue to use the neck-reining techniques which their discipline calls for, beginners should only use direct rein aids. These are applied exactly as they are astride, with light finger pressure for fine adjustments, flexion of the wrist for stronger aids (or hard mouths) and the whole forearm coming into use in emergencies. A common analogy for this is the concert pianist who uses just the fingers for tinkly pieces but the whole arm for great crashing chords. Another is a sponge full of water which will yield drips on gentle pressure or floods on hard pressure. Some teachers actually say 'sponge the reins'. A useful exercise to refine your rein use, or to teach your horse to listen to gentle aids, is to squeeze the reins in time with his footfalls, saying out loud, one word per squeeze 'Horse-here-is-my-hand'. It is rather like cadence braking when you want to stop your car without skidding.

All teachers of side-saddle are used to pupils telling them that their horse goes better side-saddle than astride. What these riders don't realise, until it is pointed out to them, is that they are actually saying that they are heavy-handed astride. Because their seat is insecure, they hang on to the reins — riding 'with the brakes on'. Once they find they are secure on the side-saddle, they relax their hands and the horse is then free to go forward without restriction.

The idea that women have lighter hands than men because they are the 'gentle sex' is another piece of Victorian nonsense. When this idea originated, all women rode side-saddle and thus did not have to hang onto the reins to stay in the saddle. You will find that as soon as you have got used to an independent seat side-saddle, you will want to achieve the same independence astride, and your riding will improve all round.

Incidentally, although hands are usually referred to in the plural, don't forget that they are actually two separate objects. You should be able to use both hands independently astride, but you need to use your right hand on its own far more often, and more delicately, when you are riding side-saddle. This is especially true in the early stages of learning, or when you have a novice horse, when the whip is needed in lieu of the right leg. A dressage whip is ideal, as it is strong enough to exert a steady pressure and 'whippy' enough for multiple taps, as well as being long enough to reach from the normal hand position to the astride position of your right heel, without you having to lower your right hand and pull yourself out of position.

## *Comfort*

The final, but vital, point about your basic position is that it should be comfortable. Obviously it will feel strange at first, but if is actually uncomfortable, there is something wrong, and in almost all cases the problem lies with the saddle. The whole essence of side-saddle is that it is a comfortable way to ride, and if you aren't comfortable when you are standing still, you should rectify it before you move off.

# 5

# Getting Moving – Walk and Trot

## *Use of Seat and Back*

The use of the seat and back side-saddle is the same as it is astride. It will feel a little different, of course, because a different part of the seat is on the saddle, but the principle is the same. Relaxed loins and lower back create a 'following' seat which allows the horse to go forward freely; 'blocking' the loins and back in a half-halt impedes his movement and tells him to 'listen' to his rider; stronger blocking and closed hands/leg/whip brings him to a good square 'ridden' halt rather than the unbalanced stop that results from mere pulling on the reins.

If you are working in a field rather than a formal manege, it is worth setting out some corner markers to form a rectangle. You will then be able to ride through a series of large and small circles as well as straight lines and will not be tempted to break out of a walk before you have consolidated the feel of your seat.

Stay on the right rein for the first few sessions, and go back to the right rein when you try your first trot. In the early stages it is very easy to relax your weight back onto your left hip, and a left bend invites you to do this. After a couple of circuits, stop and consider whether your stirrup needs adjusting. If it is too long, you may be reaching for it, and shifting your weight to the left in the process.

If it is too short, your leg will be jammed up tight under the leaping head, which can have various effects. It encourages you to grip up against the pommel, tiring your leg very quickly.

It tends to shift your weight onto the back of your left buttock, encouraging you to lean back, which lifts your right knee and loosens your purchase on the fixed head. It may shift your seat back on the left, and consequently forward on the right, which also unloosens your right knee. Or it might make you shift your seat over to the right, inviting you to lean to the left.

## Leg Aids — Use of Whip

When you give the aids with your left leg, do so as you would astride, by squeezing with the lower calf as it rests on the saddle, rather than trying to reach in with your heel. This has the effect of taking your knee off the saddle and, in extreme cases, out from under the leaping head. Nor should you bend your knee to bring your heel up behind you to give the aid, unless you are doing it deliberately in one of the lateral movements.

Your right 'leg' aids are replaced with pressure or taps from your whip, applied where your right heel would be astride. In general, a series of light taps is preferable, as it is difficult to apply pressure without opening the hand in the process and confusing the horse. Beginners do tend to worry about having to use a whip instead of their right leg, but in fact it doesn't matter if you don't use anything. Most horses accept that a squeeze from one leg applied with a relaxing of the back and hands, and possibly a click of the tongue, means that they should go forward. If necessary, just say 'walk on'.

If you do carry a whip, and are not used to doing so, just be careful that you do not tip your right hand forward so the other end of the whip goes up to tickle your horse on top of his back.

## Suppleness

You need to pay a lot of attention in the early stages to the suppleness of your back/loins, by 'following' the movement as your horse walks. If you find this difficult, do some suppling exercises with a hula hoop, for if you cannot follow the movement at the walk you will have difficulty in feeling the movements of the back legs in trot. This is important not only for rising trot, but also for accurate canter strike-offs.

You should be able to tell what each hind leg is doing through your seat and you can't develop that awareness if your seat and back are stiff.

Once you are feeling secure, and sure that your weight will not drop back to the left, you can try some work in walk on the left rein. Keep the bend gentle and keep going back to the other rein or straight lines so that you can check your position with that imaginary line down your front. When you are ready to try a trot, go back to the right rein and stay on it until you are absolutely certain that your seat is secure.

## Sitting and Rising Trot

There is no point in trying to pretend that trotting side-saddle is easy or comfortable, whether rising or sitting. Unfortunately, in today's competitions, one has to do it, so the old fashioned idea that a lady never trotted has to be abandoned.

Your very first trot should be in a straight line, with someone standing behind you watching to see if the back of your saddle moves. If it does, and tightening the balance strap does not stop it, you should not trot again until you have had the saddle fitted, or you risk scalding your horse's back.

It should also be a sitting trot, as rising trot is extremely hard work and should not be attempted until you are quite experienced. The amount of trot work you can do, and the length of each period of trot will depend on how supple you are. As long as you do not have any difficulty with sitting trot astride, you should not have any riding side-saddle.

The ideal is for your head to progress along a level 'line' always at about the same height from the ground, rather than bob up and down. Obviously this ideal is impossible to achieve, as the horse's back goes up and down, but it is possible for your body to absorb a lot of this movement. It is rather like the suspension in a car on a bumpy road — the wheels go up and down, but the car itself glides smoothly on top. Your 'shock absorbers' are your buttocks, loins and waist, but they must be supple and 'soft' to do their job. If you are generally stiff, or have made your back rigid, you will bump up and down on the saddle. By the time this jolting gets up to your neck and head it will create a whiplash-like effect which is ugly to watch as well as uncomfortable for you. It is also very uncomfortable for the horse. He will probably try to evade it by hollowing his back and throwing up his head, which makes his trot uneven and makes you bump even more.

This bumping can be likened to the shaft of a hunting whip balanced on a board. If the board is jolted up and down, the whip will bounce off the board. But if the whip is held above the board so only the thong is in contact, that thong will bend with the movement and the shaft will remain stiff. Think of your back as that whip, with your waist and hips as the thong; or, if you prefer, think of your back as a rubber column or a coiled spring.

The jolting will not only be uncomfortable, it will make you tense all over and you will probably grip up under the leaping head. Recite this mantra to yourself as you trot — 'Don't clamp on, soften the back, relax the left leg, pull the knee down with the toe...'

The opposite problem to a rigid back is that of the upper back and neck that are too soft. This causes one of the commonest riding faults astride — the bobbing head one sees so often in low-level dressage competitions. It is the result of loosening the back so much that it rounds. The pelvis tilts backwards, the ribcage drops, the shoulders come forward and the head nods in time with each step. If you have this problem, the cure is to draw yourself up while taking a deep breath, raising your diaphragm and opening up your front like a flower. Think of this as lengthening your front line; lifting your rib-cage away from your navel, or 'breathe in, pull up, stay up, breathe out', or 'up, back and down with the shoulders'.

These problems are almost entirely confined to sitting trot, but in the British show ring there is no need to rise (post) to the trot. In other countries, at some levels of dressage, and in the hunting field, it is necessary to rise. It is anyway a valuable skill to learn, as it strengthens the muscles in the right leg which will increase your ability to stay on in difficult situations. As with rising trot astride, there is no need to rise any further than necessary to ease the horse's movement, although some horses do pack more of a punch than others. But on a side-saddle, however much impetus comes from the horse, rising trot requires a muscular effort from the right leg.

Don't try rising trot until you are sufficiently sure of your basic position to be able to resume it without someone having to correct you, but do have an assistant who will stand in front and then behind to check that you are rising straight. Arrange your schooling area so that you have a long straight section and don't start rising until your horse is going straight. If you do not normally wear tights (pantyhose) when riding, it is a good idea to wear them for this exercise as they will prevent the inside of your knee getting sore. For the same reason, make sure your breeches aren't wrinkled inside your right knee.

Try a 'dry run' a couple of times with your horse standing still before you get into motion. Lock your right knee firmly on to the saddle to get a good purchase. Press your left knee and thigh firmly against the saddle, but don't press down on to the stirrup to push yourself up. Then transfer your body weight forward and back along your right thigh with a gentle rocking movement and a slight forward inclination of your body. You may incline slightly to the right, so you can just see down your horse's right shoulder. The key to all of this is that your movements should be slight, as the further you move, the more likely you are to twist or lean.

This is why you need that assistant to watch you, to make sure you are rising straight. The usual reason for a crooked rise is pushing from the stirrup or gripping up under the leaping head. Once you are sure you are rising straight, get your assistant to watch you from the nearside, to ensure that you are not rocking too enthusiastically. This can loosen your right knee and gradually work you forward on the saddle.

Three or four circuits rising on one long side is plenty for the first session, because rising trot really is hard work for both you and the horse. It would be wise to make it the last thing you do before you stop for the day, and to check the horse's back carefully to be sure the saddle hasn't rubbed him.

You should stay on the right rein until you are proficient, but then you will need to be sure you are on the correct diagonal for the bend.

# 6

# Cantering, Galloping and Jumping

Canter is the best gait side-saddle, both to watch and to ride. There is nothing quite like it, except perhaps sitting on a swimming horse but, like the other gaits, it has the potential for ugliness if performed badly.

## Aids for Canter

Many beginners are puzzled about the aids for canter, as they are accustomed to using both legs simultaneously. With walk and trot, it is easy enough to apply the left leg and a tap from the whip together, but canter requires a different action with each leg when astride. So what is the side-saddle equivalent of 'inside leg on the girth, outside leg behind the girth'?

The answer is dependent on your general riding ability, the level of schooling of your horse and, to a certain extent, the degree of precision required. The least sophisticated method is to steady your trot as you approach a corner, feel the inside rein and use your left leg on the right rein, whip on the left rein, actually at the corner. For the really sophisticated rider with a highly schooled horse, the answer is to school the horse to canter on the correct lead at the lift of the inside hand.

For those in between these two extremes, the answer is to time the aid carefully and apply a little nudge with the inside seat bone when the horse is on the outside diagonal. Since this diagonal is, of course, outside fore and inside hind on the ground, the outside hind is in the air and about to come down. The nudge from the inside tells the horse to reach a little further with that leg in the first step of canter.

Many people do not understand that the first step in a proper canter (not the unbalanced scramble one often sees) is from the outside hind. They think that because one refers to the 'leading' foreleg, it is that foreleg which takes the first canter step. If you are unsure about this, check with a book that shows the sequence of footfalls in each gait. It is an important point, for a combination of a tight corner, an unbalanced horse and a novice rider could bring the horse down.

## Common Problems in Strike-Off

Newcomers to side-saddle tend to assume that the difficult strike-off is on the left rein, because the right leg is lacking. But it is easier, if you must apply the inside leg on the girth and the outside leg behind the girth to put the left leg on forward and the whip well behind on the right, than to use the whip on the girth on the right as strongly as you need to. For this aid, taps with the whip will not do — a steady pressure is needed and that is difficult to apply on the girth without inadvertently opening the hand and thus confusing the horse. What you are actually doing, when you put your leg back astride, is saying to the horse, 'I want you to make your first canter step with *this* hind leg.' With the strategically timed nudge from the inside seat bone side-saddle, you are saying 'First canter step with *that* leg over there.'

The real problem with getting a good strike-off and continued canter on the right lead comes if your seat is not absolutely straight. If you are inclined to the left, your body weight is telling your horse to bend to the left, and it is hardly surprising that he cannot canter to the right. It is a common problem and it is often caused, astride as well as aside, by the very act of giving the aid. It is all too easy, in the process of putting your leg back, to put the whole of your body back, and then to leave it there. Even when the leg is returned to its proper place, if the upper body is still turned to the left, it is telling the horse to bend in the wrong direction.

So although it is a common problem, it is an easy one to cure. If you have difficulty with the concept, try it out for yourself on foot. Lean to the left, tip your head to the left, then try a child's 'horsey horsey' canter circle to the right. It really is extremely difficult and once you have tried it, then altered your bend and tried it again, you will have gained a valuable insight into how much influence your body alignment can have over your horse's free movement. So, back on your horse, try turning yourself exaggeratedly to the right or at the very least twitch your right shoulder back, before asking for the canter. Continue doing this until you have 'recorded' the kinaesthetic feel for the bend.

Although it may be easier to get the strike-off for left canter, you have to be even more careful of your body alignment. It is so tempting on this rein to let your weight back on the left that you can overdo the bend and your horse will obediently tighten his circles until he reaches the point where his balance fails him. So keep your circles good and large; keep your right foot turned into his shoulder; keep your right shoulder back and all should be well.

If you do not have any of these problems, how do you achieve that elegant effortless poise that is the epitome of side-saddle elegance? The secret is in that one word — effortless. The ideal is the serene rider who floats along on top of the horse and that is achieved simply by sitting still and letting your horse get on with the cantering. Many riders are far too busy in canter, niggling at the reins, using their heel or actually trying to urge the horse along with their upper body. They seem to think he will stop cantering if they don't keep on at him, but it is more likely to be this constant niggling which makes him break down into trot. If you are guilty of this, tell yourself that it is your horse's job to canter and yours to sit quietly on top and let him get on with it.

## Other Canter Problems

Sitting quietly does not mean an unmoving rigidity that impedes the horse's movement. Remember that there is a lot of power coming from the quarters in canter and also quite a lot of head movement. If you do not absorb this power and movement in your loins and hands, it will absorb you and you will move around a lot. It doesn't look elegant and it shifts the saddle and rubs your horse's back. The desirable loin movement is difficult to describe in polite, socially acceptable terms, but a classic teacher's comment is 'If you were a married lady I could tell you exactly what the movement should be!'

If you lock your hips and do not allow them to follow the horse's movement, the resultant 'rowing' of the top of your body will also affect your hands. 'Rowing' itself can also be caused by fixed hands, and you will have to give some thought to which is the cause and which the effect. Fixed hands are another very common fault, especially in the show ring, but that doesn't make them a minor fault. They are the result of interpreting 'keep your hands still' as meaning 'in relation to *your body*', rather than the correct 'in relation to *your horse's mouth*'. The place chosen side-saddle is often by the right knee. (Astride, it is just above the wither.) The horse is then unable to move his head and adopts a rocking horse motion, and the rider's shoulders sway back and forth over the pivot formed by her hands.

To correct the fault you have to manage your horse's mouth. Loosen your shoulders, elbows and wrists, then allow your horse's head to pull your hands forward a little as he dips his forehand. As he raises his forehand, you take back your hands: you allow him, then he allows you. You can imagine your hands are attached to your waist by a piece of elastic which stretches and contracts as he moves his head. Alternatively, think of the movement of your hands as a little circle — down and forward, up and back.

There is one other canter fault commonly seen in side-saddle, and that is the rider who 'screws' her body with each stride of the horse. The word 'screw' is an unfortunate one to have to use, with its vulgar connotation, but 'revolve' isn't quite the same, nor is 'rotate'. It happens when you grip up with your left thigh under the leaping head, tightening and loosening your grip with each stride. This moves the whole of your left thigh back and forth and your left hip follows. The hip movement pivots on your right seat bone and the whole of your body twists with the movement of the horse, as though you were sitting in a revolving chair and idly pushing yourself around and back with one foot.

As if this weren't bad enough, your right foot will be coming away from the saddle in time with the movement, and this is the crux of the matter. You are trying to cling to the saddle by gripping both pommels between your legs instead of using your right leg purchase to hold you on. The only solution is to go back to basics at the walk on the right rein. Take your foot out of the stirrup and let it dangle and you will soon realise that you do not need the leaping head to keep you on. After all, the leaping head wasn't invented until 1830 and ladies cantered perfectly well before then without it.

Figure 15 Correct body alignment at canter

Another less often seen canter fault is that of asking for the canter strike-off by leaning forwards and to the inside. This is actually counter productive, as it lifts your outside hip and prevents you from using your inside seat bone. If anything, your shoulders should be brought back to lighten the forehand. It is a sign of an uneducated rider, and like so many of these uneducated body movements, the real damage is done when the body is not returned to the upright but continues to lean.

Obviously in canter your body should be inclined slightly inwards, but not beyond the angle of the horse's plane. You should not need to do anything yourself to create this inclination, it will come from the inclination of horse and saddle. In other words, when viewed from behind, your body should always make a right angle with the top of the saddle. If you lean in or out, this right angle will be broken. The same applies to the view from the side. You don't help your horse in canter by learning forward, you just encourage him onto his forehand and he will appear to be dragging himself down into the ground. He will also be unable to give you a balanced downwards transition, but will fall forwards into a nasty jolting trot.

## *Galloping*

Galloping does require you to shift your weight and hands forward. For showing, this need only be slight, perhaps with your hands advanced as far as your knee, then, when you are approaching a corner and you want to slow down and balance, all you need do is to bring your shoulders and hands back to their normal position. For hunting, or other situations where you expect a long gallop, you will want to get your weight well forward. There is no need to lift your seat from the saddle, but you should tip your seat bones forward and bring your shoulders forward over your knee. Your hands can go in front of the wither and you could even rest them on your horse's shoulders.

In neither situation should you lengthen the reins by letting them slip through your hands. Your horse has all the freedom he needs when you put your hands forward and if you need to pull up in a hurry all you have to do is sit up and draw back

Figure 16 Hands and body in the gallop. The horse has all the head freedom he needs but the rider has only to straighten up to bring him back in an emergency

your hands.

Whenever you gallop, be sure you consciously lock your right leg on. If your horse trips or pecks at speed and you have omitted to lock on, you can neither help your horse nor prevent yourself falling.

## Jumping

The same consideration applies to jumping. It is the right leg that keeps you in the saddle when jumping, not the left leg jammed up under the leaping head. Just because it is called 'leaping' head does not mean you have to use it when leaping. Its purpose is to hold you in the saddle in the sort of emergency that would otherwise tip you forward and 'out of the front door' — and it just so happens that this sort of emergency is more likely to happen when you are jumping.

If you consider the hazards that tip the astride rider forwards, with the exception of clumsy horses who stumble and naughty horses who buck, you will realise they are mostly associated with jumping — refusals, pecks on landing, 'cat' jumps, etc. With all of these, the effect side-saddle is that you slide forward until you come up against the leaping head, and there you stop. If you have gripped up when you realise there is a problem,

Figure 17 Poor jumping position

a   legs off the saddle, hands pulled in and elbows stuck out. Rider is too far forward and is unsafe if the horse pecks or trips on landing

b  hands in air, left leg back

your slide will be shortened, but if you grip up all the time you may twist your seat and the jolt will swing you off the saddle.

Popping over a few jumps in a Ladies Working Hunter class will not damage your left thigh if you grip up for each jump, but if you do it throughout a day's hunting you will soon develop a badly bruised and swollen leg. And it is just not necessary over most jumps. It is not until the fences go up over 4 ft (1.3 m) that anything else is needed.

c leaning backwards and sideways, 'straphanging' on reins

This applies to right leg, left leg, seat-bones and for that matter, the saddle itself. There was a theory in the 1930s that jumping side-saddle required the rider to 'get well forward' and a special saddle was designed with its leaping head very close to the fixed head to allow this. But we now know that it is not necessary unless you are showjumping or hunting over very big fences. If you doubt this, look at any of the pre-war books on side-saddle and you will see, that with the exception of Archer–Houblon, seats are firmly in the saddle over fences.

Even so, many saddles do have an alternative position for the leaping head, so the option is there if you do need it.

It is neither necessary, nor desirable, to shorten the stirrup, as this does jam your leg up under the leaping head. It also encourages you to bend your knee and raise your left heel, which is liable to be unpopular with your horse if that heel is adorned with a spur!

Although you are far less likely to have a fall side-saddle than astride, you should wear a proper hard hat with a safety harness for jumping lessons. You should not wear an apron, as your teacher or assistant should be able to see your feet. It is not only the left foot that tends to be displaced − nervous riders tend to lift their right toe and tense their right knee up off the saddle. Before you try anything over fences or even poles on the ground, practise your position while your horse is standing.

The correct position for jumping side-saddle is called the 'fold' because it consists of folding forward from the hips. With your seat firmly on the saddle, fold forward with your back straight and your hands leading to allow your horse to stretch his neck. Let your hands go up his neck by his mane (one either side) and allow the angle of your elbows to open up. Don't throw the reins at your horse, just let your hands go forward more than your body, but maintain a good contact. Then, as your horse lands and you return your body to the upright, your hands can come smoothly back to their normal position. A common fault with inexperienced riders is that they bring their hands in towards their stomach as they fold, turning their elbows out in the process. They then wonder why their horse stops!

Your spine must remain parallel to your horse's spine and neck and you should keep your eyes on where you are going. If you must look down, it should be to the right rather than the left. Your fold should be forwards, not over your legs to the left. This could unbalance your horse and if he jumps big it is liable to jolt your seat round so you end up facing left. Whether or not this happens, it will move your right knee forwards away from the fixed head and you will have nothing on which to get a purchase. All this shifting round may upset

Figure 18 A good position for jumping. The horse has all the head and neck freedom he needs, but the rider can easily bring him back if he pecks on landing

your horse enough to make him buck you off when he lands.

Your folding action should be smooth. Obviously, the higher the jump, the further you will need to fold, but it must still be smooth. If you 'snap' forward and mistime it as your horse rises into his jump you will get at the least a painful thump on your left breast from the fixed head and at the worst a cracked rib. Equally, your return to the upright on landing should be smooth, especially where your hands are concerned. If you bang your horse in the teeth when he lands he will soon go off the idea of jumping.

American riders do tend to get much further forward than British riders when jumping astride, and may want to move the leaping head. Even so, you should not try to get too far forward side-saddle as it is easy to 'get in front of' the saddle and very difficult to get back again. As a general rule, anything which moves the right knee forward is dangerous, so this is a situation where style should be modified a little in the interests of safety.

Timing your fold is much the same as it would be astride. Too soon and your weight goes onto your horse's forehand just as he is trying to lift it off the ground; too late and you will be left behind, bounced off your seat by his take-off spring and landing with a bump that jars you and your horse's back — and probably his mouth as well.

The best way to guard against this is to go back to the classic way of teaching jumping astride, with poles on the ground. Walk over them first, then trot, then add a low cavaletti at the end. Start with low jumps and gradually work your way up to higher ones. The distances between trotting poles, ground line poles and jump, and a series of jumps is exactly the same as it would be astride. The only difference is that a course of jumps should not involve any tight left turns, and in the early stages, no left turns at all.

# 7

# Advanced Matters

*Refining Your Performance* _____

What we have considered so far are the basics of riding side-saddle. Now we need to consider refining your performance and adding some more advanced movements. Most riders seek such refinements for competitive purposes, but it is worth mentioning that your pleasure in merely riding around the countryside will be enhanced if your horse is responsive and balanced.

Comparative newcomers to riding are often uncertain as to whether their horse is balanced. Apart from a tendency to jerk or 'fall' from one gait to another, lack of balance is most often evidenced by unrhythmic movement. This is not a problem of side-saddle, but one of an unschooled horse, and the exercises normally used to educate the horse astride can be applied equally well aside. We haven't room here to describe all these exercises, but there are a couple of lungeing exercises which even a novice rider can use.

The first is to lunge him in trot on a slope. He will lose his balance downhill at first, and break into canter, but if you persevere he will soon learn to balance himself and trot all the way. The other, also in trot, is to lunge him in a series of spirals. Start with a big circle, then shorten the rein gradually to a small circle, then gradually let it out again. At the beginning of this exercise, your horse will not be able to cope with small circles and you should let him out again when he begins to have difficulty. You will do more harm than good if you insist

61

on small circles when he is not ready for them, but if you persevere you will soon find he can cope with a really small circle.

His problem (and yours) may be a lack of concentration brought on by boredom. You see this in riding-school horses, who spend their working lives going round and round the outside of the manege. Keep your horse's attention by constantly changing the shape you are riding – start with a big circle, then a smaller one, then a circuit of the whole manege, then small circles in opposite corners, or loops, figures of eight – all of this adds interest without having to change gait and lose your steady rhythm. The only thing about doing this side-saddle is that, as always, you should avoid tight left-handed turns and circles.

Why not play some appropriate music while you are working? Appropriate, in this case, means music with a rhythm which matches your horse's ideal rhythm in the gait you are working in. Music does make it easier to maintain a steady pace all the way round, especially if your horse tends to slow down for corners and rush along the straights. If closing your hands and blocking down with your seat does not steady these rushes, you may need to lean back a little to check the speed as you come out of the corner.

If you have ongoing problems with maintaining a rhythm, it may be your problem rather than the horse's. Quite a lot of people have this problem, and it often comes from having been encouraged to walk too early as a baby. 'Too early' in this context is not a measurement of time from birth, but relates to a failure to go through the crawling process properly. Crawling is part of our brain programming for proper movement and babies who skip that stage in their development tend to grow into people with poor ability to detect and maintain good rhythm. Such people tend to crawl laterally; that is, left leg and left arm move together, instead of doing the correct 'cross-crawl' where left leg and right arm move together. If you suspect you have this problem, get down on your hands and knees and check it out. It is quite easy to cure – just practice cross-crawling every day for a few weeks.

Going back to the problem of the horse who rushes out of

corners and the way to steady him, it should be mentioned that you have to be careful not to overdo this. Apply the correction gently, not in a hurry, or your horse will stop as though he had run into a wall. Side-saddle gives you tremendous stopping power, far more than even a man astride, as many a big horse has found when he tried it on with what he thought was a frail female rider. The old horse dealer's standard cure for a puller or a bucker was to ride it side-saddle to teach it what brakes were, and in extreme cases they would even hook the reins under the leaping head and pull upwards!

The mechanisms of this are that it is extremely difficult to set your seat firmly enough astride to use your lower back and hands against a puller. Aside it is much easier: lock your right leg on firmly, bring your seat forward and brace your back; at the same time bend your elbows and bring your hands in to your stomach. If necessary, turn your hands over with your knuckles underneath, adding the strength of your clenched fist and biceps to the reins.

This is also a position of unshiftability, which may be useful if you find yourself on an idle horse who thinks he can ignore light touches of leg and whip. Nagging with heel and whip is counterproductive in this situation, for such a horse soon learns to ignore this. It is far better to lock on and ready yourself for fireworks, then give him one really good whack to show him that you really do mean business.

## Extended Trot

While you will hopefully not need to use these extremes, it is valuable to develop the strength and sensitivity of your lower back by practising half-halts. Whether for showing or dressage, you will eventually want to work on extensions, and your lower back is an important part of the aids for these. It is not wise to practise extension on a horse who is new to side-saddle. He needs time to develop his back muscles for the basic task of carrying the heavier saddle and the backward placement of the rider before you ask him to exert those muscles in extending. At best he will react by flattening his back and running with his hocks out behind him; at worst he could

strain his back. This is a major problem with British show
ponies who tend automatically to switch on their daisy-cutter
action whenever trot is called for, and it is the reason you see
them dropping their backs in the line-up.

With the horse who does not already extend, probably the
best way to achieve it is coming out of a small circle on to a
straight line. As always in side-saddle, start off on the right
rein, as you do not want the slightest hint of imbalance to give
conflicting signals. Build up impulsion during the circle then,
as you straighten up to go down the long side, drive that
impulsion with your seat onto your hands. You may need to
lift and separate your hands and lean back a little. What you
must not do is drop or relax your hands forward, as this allows
all the impulsion to escape as your horse drops his head. Do
not lean forward, as this prevents you driving with your seat
and puts your weight onto the forehand, preventing your
horse from collecting himself and lifting his forehand.

In the early stages many horses break into a canter as they
come out of the circle. If this happens check back to trot, circle
and try again with your hands well separated. Time the use of
your leg/whip very carefully so that it does not fall on the
outside diagonal and thus cannot be interpreted as a canter
aid. When you succeed, do not reward your horse by relaxing
your hands, as this will allow the impulsion to 'fall out the
front door'. Nor should you drop your hands when the desired
passage of extension is complete, as your horse may fall onto
his forehand in unbalance instead of reverting to ordinary trot.

## Transitions

Another area that frequently needs care to avoid this unbalanced
fall onto the forehand is that of both upward and downward
transitions. Even in ordinary showing classes, where the judge
is not particularly concerned with transitions as such, it takes
precious time to balance and collect after a poor transition, and
the judge may get a bad impression of your horse's paces
in the meantime. In dressage and equitation classes, good
transitions are essential.

The requirements for a good transition side-saddle are

the same as for astride – balance, attention from the horse, and a precisely timed and accurate aid. Most bad downward transitions, especially from canter to trot, are caused by failing to balance your horse first, then 'throwing the reins at him' so that he falls into a jolting uneven trot. Coming down from canter is not just a matter of stopping cantering but a matter of going from canter to a properly controlled trot. The same applies to the trot/walk transition. Your horse should stop trotting and start walking properly, not fall into a sloppy shamble. Use a half-halt after the initial balancing, brace your back slightly and close your hands to achieve the change of pace, then relax your hands and drive with your seat and leg/whip.

Upward transitions can be marred by over-enthusiastic half-halts or by tension in the back. There is little point in giving an aid to go forward with your seat and legs if the upper part of your body then impedes free forward movement. If you bring your shoulders back and keep them there with your back rigid, your horse will hollow his back and throw his head up in protest. If you find yourself tensing up, make a point of breathing out during transitions as it is difficult to remain tense as you do so.

## Accuracy of Shapes

The next area to refine is accuracy of shape. Probably the most common comments from dressage and equitation judges relate to inaccuracy of obligatory patterns, and even in freestyle tests, you hear judges saying 'Is that meant to be a straight line or a loop?' A certain amount of inaccuracy in circles is due to the circle being too small for the horse's balancing ability and the rider trying to sort him out when he has swung his quarters out, but more often the fault is with the rider who moves her body around.

## Contra-Body Rotation

There is a concept called 'contra-body rotation', which is based on the theory that the rider's hips control the horse's hips and the rider's shoulders control the horse's shoulders. When applied properly, turning your shoulders by rotating at the waist will make your horse turn in the same direction without your needing to do anything with your hands. When you add to this the fact that any horse will put himself underneath you if you shift your weight, you will find that you can produce perfect level turns, as though your horse were on rails. This is particularly useful with a horse who tends to drift sideways round corners, leading with his inside shoulder.

Try this exercise. In walk, change the rein across the centre of the manege by riding two right angles connected by a straight line. The first time, just make the turns by your usual method and concentrate on how your horse feels as he makes each turn. Then do it again but this time, as you approach the point where you would give the signal to turn, do not do anything with your hands or leg/whip but rotate your upper body from the waist through a right angle to face the way you want to go. Your horse will turn underneath you and as he does so, you rotate back to face front, then the other way to change the rein at the other side. The fact that this works, almost like magic, is a revelation that constitutes a high 'cliff' for most riders.

It doesn't work if your hips turn as well (this makes the quarters swing) or if you lean in when you rotate. The rotation must be from your waist and with your shoulders level, and you must allow your arms and hands to accompany your shoulders or your horse will not be able to use his neck properly. Think about it — all the time his neck is straight, the rein-to-lap distance will be the same on either side. If he is to turn his head in the direction of the turn, the inside rein shortens and the outside rein lengthens. By allowing your hands to 'go with' your shoulders, keeping your shoulder/arm and elbow angles more or less constant, your outside hand goes forward and your inside hand comes back, giving your horse the freedom to bend his neck as he needs.

Do this exercise several times in walk, then repeat it from the beginning in trot. Now you are ready to add the final piece. Ride it again, but as you start the turn, after rotating your body, shift your weight onto your inside hip (without leaning in). The instruction for this when astride is 'Shift your pelvis across and step onto your inside stirrup but be careful not to collapse at the waist.' This produces another revelation: your horse levels himself to carry your weight in its new position and he goes round the corner level instead of tilting to the inside — and this is what makes the difference in producing accurate circles and corners.

What you now have to do is refine your body movements, and your horse's acceptance of them, down from the big shifts necessary when you first try this exercise to the least possible movement needed to produce the effect. The same consideration applies to all your aids. The ideal is the horse who moves beautifully beneath his rider without her seeming to move at all. Only a skilled eye should be able to detect your tiny shoulder shrugs, seat nudges and fingers quivering on the reins. Watch a film of the Spanish Riding School and see how infinitesimal the riders' body movements are.

## Lateral Work, Indirect Rein of Opposition

This principle of big movements to start and refining them later also applies to lateral work, as does the principle of the rider's shoulder/hips controlling the horse's shoulders/quarters. The novice rider believes that the secret of lateral movements lies in putting a leg back to push the quarters over. Since the side-saddle rider has no leg on the right but only a whip which seems inadequate to 'push', she searches for an alternative answer. Ignorant of the use of bodyweight and sideways nudges of the seat, she falls back on the mantra 'right indirect rein of opposition behind the withers'. The rein of opposition *is* useful side-saddle, but it is by no means the whole answer to controlling the quarters.

Many people are confused about the indirect rein of opposition. To understand it, you have to go right back to basics. Consider the horse, as viewed from above, when it forms approximately a rectangle. (It tapers at the front, but that is irrelevant for the purpose of this discussion.) Taking the nose as the front, the centre point of this rectangle is just behind the front legs. Taking that centre point as our axis, our stride aids take the form of making the rectangle swing round that axis.

Pulling or pushing one corner affects the whole animal, not just that corner − pulling or pushing the front in one direction causes the rear to move in the opposite direction, hence the expression 'rein of opposition to the quarters'.

You can demonstrate this by taking a rectangular piece of paper and poking a pencil through the middle. Mark it to show which is the front, then pull the right-front corner (pull the right rein) and watch the whole thing spin until you stop it by pulling the left front or pushing the left rear. This right rein is the direct rein. You can achieve the same effect by pushing the left front (laying the left rein on the horse's neck, or neck reining). This is the indirect rein, applied in front of the wither. Both of which are fine if you want the rectangle to spin round its axis. You can also get it to spin clockwise by pushing the right-rear corner (right leg back).

But what if you want the rectangle not to spin, but to move bodily to the left? Then you must either push back and front on the same side simultaneously (right rein used on the neck and right leg back) or, since non-stock seat (Western) riding disciplines do not use the neck rein, you must pull one side at the front and push the other side at the back (left direct rein and right leg back). But you can't do that side-saddle because you haven't got a right leg to put back. What about the whip? Fine, it serves as a leg, but only if a tap will suffice, because if you start applying any pressure on the bottom of the whip with your hand in its usual position you run the risk of also applying the right direct rein and starting the spin. But if you bring the right hand well back and down a little, and apply it backwards and inwards, you are using it as a push on the rear rather than a pull on the front − and that is the indirect rein of opposition behind the wither.

It works, but it is not easy to apply finely. And with the rider who can use the rest of her body finely, the same effect can be obtained without it. We'll come back to that in a minute though, because we haven't quite finished with that right hand. What about moving to the right? Easy, the novice thinks, because I have a left leg to push with. Wrong − it's not that easy. Yes, there is a left leg to push with at the back, but you also need to pull the front to the right and since, on a side-saddle, the right hand is already behind the wither you have to be careful how you use it if it is not to be interpreted by the horse as that indirect rein. You must either advance the right rein, which you can't do without putting your weight forward, or use your right leg.

'What right leg?' you will be asking. 'I haven't got a right leg!' Oh yes you have — it is resting on your horse's left shoulder and you can use the foot to tap those shoulders to the right. No more than a tap, as a harder pressure might move your hips.

What of the other ways to influence the quarters — or the front for that matter? There is always a risk that rein aids will start a swing or a neck bend, unless they are carefully applied and steadied by the other rein, in a constant balancing act. There are also risks in trying to *push* the horse to one side. The fact is that you cannot push him anywhere, certainly not with one leg when you are on top. A strong man on the ground cannot push a horse sideways if he does not wish to go. Any attempt to do so will only end up in a mess, with you tense and frustrated and your horse confused.

You can't push him. But you can teach him to move away from a touch on his side, whether the touch is from a leg, or a whip, or — and no one ever thinks of this — from the balance strap. It doesn't work with the short type of balance strap sewn onto the girth, but a separate balance strap rests on your horse's side in more or less the place where you would be putting your right leg. If you nudge the saddle with your right seatbone, the balance strap is pressed on his side. And of course the seatbone nudge is another aid that he moves away from, as well as the leg pressure.

The final point to remember is that, as mentioned in the contra body rotation exercise, your horse will instinctively place himself under your weight if you move it to one side. A quick application of weight on a turn will level him up, a prolonged application will encourage him actually to step under your weight. You just have to be careful that you are placing your weight rather than applying pressure with it. Your horse will put himself under placed weight but move away from pressure, whether that pressure is a nudge or prolonged. Placing your weight can turn into pressing, if your pelvic shift is followed by a collapse or by top body rotation. This is why the dropped left hip with its accompanying left shoulder back makes the horse carry his quarters to the right.

What all of this means is that if you aspire to ride advanced movements on a side-saddle you will have to develop considerable fine and accurate control of your own body. If you are already riding these movements creditably astride you will already have that control, and will be able to adapt your stride aids for side-saddle. If you have never ridden these movements before, you should do so for the first time on an experienced horse, for if you do not know what the movement should feel like, how will you know whether you are doing it properly?

## Canter from Halt or Rein-Back

One of the compulsory movements in the Side-Saddle Association's UK Equitation Championships which causes a lot of grief is canter from halt or rein-back. Many competitors wrongly interpret this as meaning that a few strides of walk and trot are permissible. This is understandable where a completely novice rider is concerned, but a moderately competent rider in any discipline should take it for granted that her horse will instantly obey a precisely given aid. If you give the aid for canter on a particular rein, your horse should canter on that rein, regardless of what he was doing before.

The more your canter aid concentrates on a lift of the inside hand the better, as this is the finest and least visible of all the aids; and as it does away with use of leg and seat, it avoids confusion when rein-back is involved. With the exception of dressage tests, there is no reason why a click of the tongue should not also be part of your aid for the canter.

To canter from halt, first ensure the halt itself is a good square one. Give the aid for a half-halt to warn your horse that you are about to give another instruction, then give your aid for the canter. This is actually more difficult than cantering from rein-back, where you change the direction of movement in a 'bounce' that provides the impulsion for canter.

Rein-back should not be attempted side-saddle until your

horse has done sufficient work side-saddle to develop his back muscles, as a mistake with thrown-up head and hollowed back could cause a serious strain. For the same reason it should not be attempted on a horse who habitually evades the bit by throwing up his head.

In the early stages, you may need an assistant to stand in front of your horse and push his nose back while you apply the aids and you both say 'Back!' The aids themselves are the same as those used astride — a request for forward movement, prevented by the firm but gentle action of the hands, which leaves no alternative but a backward movement. You may need to use the rein in opposition behind the wither to prevent his quarters swinging. It may help if you teach him astride that when you put your legs on and move them forwards you mean 'forward' and when you move them backwards you mean 'back'. He will accept this from the single leg side-saddle to mean the same thing.

## *Flying Changes*

And what about flying changes? Well, I actually told you how to do them above. You teach your horse that when you give the aid to canter on a particular rein he does it immediately, regardless of what he was doing before. This time, he will have been cantering on the other rein, and your canter aid will tell him to change. Obviously you shouldn't expect perfect changes straight away, but the principle really is that simple. Equally obviously, you will give the aid to change at a place where there is room to sort yourself out if it goes wrong, and it would also be sensible to start by changing from left rein to right.

A good way to practise changes is to canter left round half of the manege, then ask for the change on the centre line, so you can perform a big right canter circle. But be warned — horses who are not used to flying changes do tend to want to do them all the time, interpreting any slight change of bend as the aid to change and often adding a couple of bucks for good measure!

# 8

# Dress

There is a lot of traditional etiquette attached to side-saddle outfits and you should be aware that many of the 'old school' of judges will look down their noses at you if you infringe it.

## For Lessons

For lessons, apart from the obvious considerations of safety and comfort, your instructor will want to be able to see what you are doing with your body. A competent teacher can see what you are doing with your legs and feet under an apron, but it makes it that much easier if you do not wear one, and it is also easier to make adjustments to leg positions and stirrup length.

## Boots, Spurs

Ordinary breeches or jodhpurs are all that is needed, although you need to give a little extra thought to your right leg. A loose fitting boot is a nuisance as, since there is no stirrup to stop it, it will tend to slip and distract you. This is a particular hazard with wellington boots so, although many people do like them for casual wear, they are not a good idea in this situation. The other danger with wellington boots is that they do not have a proper heel and can slip through the stirrup and trap your foot. For this reason alone you should wear riding boots with a definite heel.

Long boots should not be so long in the leg that they dig

into the inside or back of your right knee, which will be bent more side-saddle than astride. When ladies rode exclusively side-saddle, their boots were made with the right leg shorter than the left so if you intend to do a lot of side-saddle you might like to think of this. You will need to rotate the garter strap on the right boot to the front, so that the buckle does not catch on the saddle and damage it.

Some competition rules specify that a spur must be worn, but you should not need one for lessons. It is certainly not advisable to wear one until your seat is really secure. If you need to apply your emergency grip, and inadvertently do so by raising your left heel, your horse will prefer you to do so without a spur!

## Breeches and Outerwear

Before modern stretch materials were invented, ladies' breeches were individually made to ensure a snug fit round the right knee. Now, all that is necessary is to ensure that there are no wrinkles to pinch or rub. The thighs should be fairly close fitting, partly to avoid rubs and partly to allow your apron to sit properly.

Whatever you choose to wear on top, be it shirt, jumper or jacket, it should also be fairly snug fitting. Until your seat is established, your instructor will want a clear view of your pelvis, spine and shoulders, so don't obstruct this view with loose jumpers or anoraks.

You should not need to be told to wear protective headgear, but quite apart from all the usual reasons, the depth of a side-saddle and your sitting position puts your head much higher than astride which means you are more vulnerable to low branches.

## Underwear

You can avoid the problem of a sore right knee by wearing tights (pantyhose) under your breeches until the tender skin behind the knee has hardened a little. Some ladies always wear tights, but for hygienic reasons this is not really a good idea in hot weather. You should also avoid panties with elasticated legs, as the weight on your right hip can be painful.

You will also need a good brassiere, particularly if you are fullbreasted. Some riders try to hide their bosom by hunching their shoulders, but this affects your balance and makes it impossible to sit properly. Fashionable 'soft shape' bras are no good for riding. They allow the breasts to lollop and that hurts! The author had this problem, and after much experimentation with 'sports' bras and others, found that the answer was a 'cross your heart' bra, which gives good support and has the added advantage of straps which do not constantly slip off the shoulders.

## Hacking

Although there is no reason why you should not hack out without an apron, you will probably feel you should wear one. Don't fall for the fallacy that you need to get your horse used to the feel of an apron on his side, in case it frightens him. When Victorian ladies wore long trailing skirts that flapped round their horses' legs this might have been a problem, but it is not now. Modern aprons are neat and short and will feel no different to your horse than the rugs he is used to wearing. For hacking the apron need not match your jacket, but for all other occasions except jumping competitions at local shows it must match.

## Habits, Waistcoats, Gloves

If you can only afford one habit and want to wear a top hat, the habit must be black. Otherwise your habit could be navy blue or very dark grey. If you can afford more than one habit, brown or grey tweed are useful, or for informal summer wear, beige or mid-grey in a lightweight fabric such as gabardine are acceptable. Any other colour, for any purpose other than fancy-dress classes or musical rides will cause judges to look down their noses and mutter 'Not suitable!' You will gain a reputation as a rank amateur or a show-off if you wear such colours.

74

Your habit should be worn with a waistcoat (vest) which may be a discreet check, canary yellow, dove grey or scarlet. Juniors as well as adults should wear long boots. You will need leather gloves, although yellow string gloves are acceptable for hunting. In 'Corinthian' classes in the United States, you must carry string 'rain' gloves under your saddle flap as well as wearing leather gloves. (These rain gloves must be put under the flap in a way which allows you to draw them out and put them on easily — which means with the fingers to the front, thumbs upwards, and right glove on the outside.) Gloves must never be black — mainly for etiquette (black gloves signify mourning, and ladies in mourning should not do anything as frivolous as ride a horse!) but also because dressage judges think it is an attempt to hide the hands and thus pay them extra attention.

In some competitions in the USA and Canada, breeches must be of the same fabric as the habit, but otherwise they need not be. However, they should be the same colour as the habit, as it is a real giveaway when you lose your perfect position and yellow breeches peep out from under your apron.

## Hats and Veils, Hair

The area of dress where most confusion arises is the correct combination of habit colour, hat and neckwear. Juniors may wear a hunting cap (always with the ribbons sewn up) or a bowler, but *never* a top hat. The hunting cap may match their habit in colour, and long hair should be in one or two plaits with discreet ribbons. Short hair must be in a net. A collar and tie must be worn.

Bowler hats (derbies) are usually black and can be worn with any colour of habit. The only other colour which is acceptable is brown and then only with a brown or brown tweed habit and only if worn with brown boots. This is known in hunting circles as 'ratcatcher' and it is the only time when an adult lady may wear a collar and tie in the hunting field.

In the show-ring in the UK, whatever the class and whether adult or junior, if a bowler hat is worn it must be with collar and tie, and hair in a bun, even if this means sewing a false bun onto the back of the hat. Top hats are for formal occasions only, and this means that the whole turnout of you and your horse must be formal. Your habit must be black, you must wear a white stock and a spur, and your horse must be plaited and in a double bridle. Although the old rule that top hats should only be worn at Royal shows has been relaxed, they are still only worn after lunch. Traditionally minded judges do not approve of short dressage toppers for side-saddle. If you have to wear one, remove the ribbon trim at the back. In the UK, a top hat should always be worn with a veil, and adults wearing bowlers should also wear a veil. (The Side-Saddle Association now considers that juniors need not wear veils with bowlers in equitation classes.) Many shows in the UK now insist that competitors in all classes must wear British Standard safety hats with a chin harness.

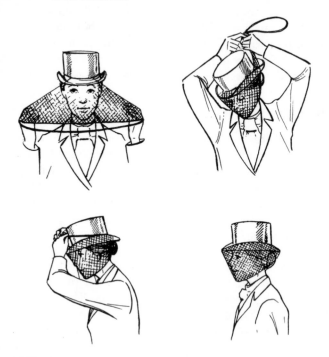

Figure 19 Putting on the veil. Hair pins into the bun will adjust any hint of bagginess

# *Hunting*

In the hunting field, unless in ratcatcher, adult ladies always wear a stock. Top hats are only worn in the proper season, not for cubbing. You should only wear one if you are a subscriber or member, but of course you can also wear it when you are a guest of another hunt. Strictly speaking, top hats should only be worn by married ladies. Traditional etiquette makes no mention of divorcees!

## *Jewellery, Buttonholes*

Earrings should be no more than tiny gold studs. 'Sleeper' rings are dangerous as they may catch on twigs. No other jewellery should be worn except a plain gold stockpin and a club badge. Even plain wedding bands are dangerous near horses. The only acceptable buttonhole in the UK is the traditional blue cornflower.

In the USA and Canada, although the basics of the above apply to Hunt or Saddle Seat classes, the detailed requirements can vary in different classes. Obviously everything is different in western classes. Do be sure to check the rule books or the International Side-Saddle Organisation's chart for each class. Please do not denigrate side-saddle by dressing like a Christmas tree, even in fancy-dress classes.

## *More Information on Habits*

If you have someone to help you, it is a good idea to put your apron on after you are mounted. This prevents it from dragging out of position and picking up hairs. A few hairs are unavoidable, but a roll of sellotape, judiciously applied, will remove them before you go into the ring. Your assistant should also make sure that your jacket seam is straight, or you may lose marks for sitting crookedly when you are not.

The waistband of the apron will have a line of cross stitches, and it is this point which should be in the front centre of your waist, not the thigh-top seam. The bottom hem of the apron must be parallel to the ground, and the back and thigh pieces

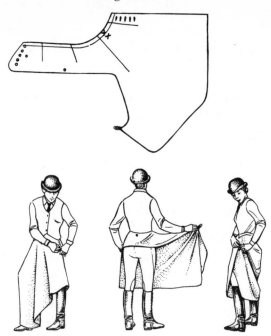

Figure 20  Putting on the apron

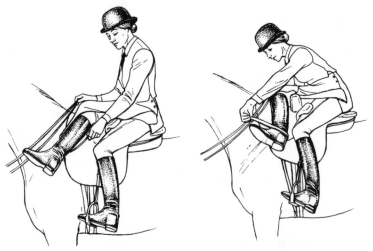

Figure 21  Adjusting the apron, putting elastic over the right foot

Figure 22 Correct length of apron

must touch the saddle at the back and offside. Your right foot should not be visible, but equally you should not have a great flap of apron hanging down below this foot. Remember that the apron footstrap goes behind your ankle before it goes over your toe, or you run the risk of your toe sticking out. If you have to replace this strap, remember that it has a deliberate twist in it.

If you want to make your own habit, you need to be aware of two essentials. The first is that the front corners of the jacket must be cut away, or it will not sit properly over your thigh. (Impecunious show pony mums often stitch back the corners of an ordinary show jacket.) The second is that the correct hang of the apron can only be achieved by thick, heavy hems,

Figure 23 Cut away jackets

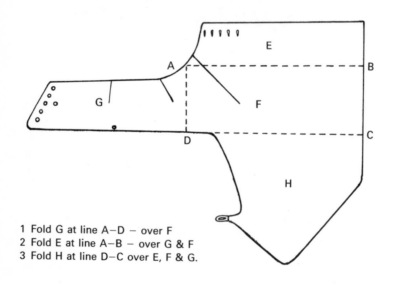

1 Fold G at line A–D – over F
2 Fold E at line A–B – over G & F
3 Fold H at line D–C over E, F & G.

Figure 24 How to fold the apron for travelling

both along the bottom edge and down the drop from the left hip. Properly tailored habits have a 6 inch (15 cm) hem. You could use buckram or a strip of melton inside the hem but not curtain weights. These never look right, and can frighten a nervous horse by banging on his side.

Figure 24 shows you how to fold your apron. This is simple when you know how, but one of those things you would never work out on your own. Start by holding the apron, outside facing you, by the top buttonhole and the place where the waist portion reaches the thigh seam. What you are looking for here is a straight line between your hands, parallel to the bottom hem. Then you flap the back piece away from you, fold the calf piece in over that, then fold the left 'drop' on top, and you have a neat, if bulky, rectangle that can be hung on a hanger or folded once more to go in a suitcase and which arrives at its destination uncreased. You can do the whole thing on a table, but it is worth practising it without, since tables are rarely available at shows.

# 9

# Competing

## General

There are no competitions in the UK where you cannot ride side-saddle. There are a few in the USA and Canada where the rules state that you may not do so, so be sure to check the rule books. Otherwise, all that matters is whether you will put yourself at a disadvantage by doing so.

In the UK, while there are no rules that say you may not ride side-saddle, this does not mean that you can assume no one will object. Some judges may feel that it is inappropriate for the class and either refuse to judge you or just ignore you. (This is most likely to happen in 'best rider' classes.) So unless you have prior knowledge of the judge, it is wise, and also polite, to check before going into the ring.

You should always have a cross-saddle with you for non-side-saddle classes where the judge rides your horse, even if it is a lady whom you know does ride aside. In a situation where she is making comparisons between the feel of different horses, she may not want to add the difference between cross and side-saddles to her deliberations. All you need do is ask if she wants you to change saddles. Although it is not unknown for a male judge to climb up onto a side-saddle, it is so rare that you should change saddles automatically.

## Showing

It is not necessary to be a Side-Saddle Association or International Side-Saddle Organisation member in order to compete in show classes, but there are advantages for members. The first is that many shows have special rosettes or trophies for members. You do not necessarily have to win the class to be eligible for these — they are for the highest placed member, so you could miss an ordinary rosette but still get a side-saddle one. The second advantage is annual Performance Awards competitions, which give points for competitions ridden side-saddle. The higher the place, the more points you get, but even if you are not placed in the class you can still build up your points score. Check the rule books for details and requirements.

For showing classes, where it is the horse that is judged rather than the rider, there are few differences between competing stride or side. The only advice one can give is to be sure that you wear what the rule books or local custom require; and to adapt the obligatory movements to show your horse off to best advantage, if his schooling and balance affects transitions and left circles.

Otherwise, it is just a matter of being professional. One often hears amateurs complain about the fact that professional showing people win more often than not, and suggesting that some unfair advantage is at work. This is absolute nonsense — the reason professionals win is that their livelihood depends on their doing so, and therefore they pay scrupulous attention to detail and practise until their performance is as close to perfection as they can get it. Amateurs who want to win will only do so by adopting the same attitude.

It should go without saying that your horse should be the right type for the class. That applies to any showing situation, but what is especially important for side-saddle classes is that your horse should have a good shoulder and free-going action that does not jolt the rider. It is the first thing that judges look for in a side-saddle horse and the lack of it is the thing that will make them reject him, even if everything else about him is perfect.

The actual techniques of ring-craft vary little in side-saddle classes from those ridden astride, but there are a couple of points that need a little extra attention. The first of these is that side-saddle is meant to be elegant. You will spoil the picture if you slump, so sitting beautifully upright must be a priority.

The other point is the business of where to carry your right hand. As mentioned in chapter 4, some showing people think a low right hand 'lengthens the horse's front line'. If you share this opinion, be careful that the tensions of competing do not lead you to stiffen your elbow and wrist, and thus impede your horse's movement. The safest rule is only to drop your hand when you first enter the ring at the walk, and even then, only on the right rein.

## Dressage

The only differences between dressage astride and side are that you must tell the secretary in advance if you intend to ride side, and that you may carry a whip in lieu of your right leg. Otherwise, everything else is the same. If the test requires rising trot, you must rise. If it does not specify, you may sit. You may ride side at any level.

## Jumping

For jumping competitions, while there is no bar to riding side and it is very laudable to promote the idea that you can do anything side-saddle that you can do astride, it is really not sensible for serious show-jumping. Against the clock there is a risk element in tight left-handed turns; and where really high fences are involved, it is difficult to get far enough forward to allow your horse full freedom of movement. This does not mean you will not get round, but you are unlikely to do so fast enough to beat good stride competitors.

If you are competing under BSJA rules, you must comply with their turn-out requirements, which basically means a white tie and white breeches.

You could also compete across country side-saddle, but where speed is crucial you could be disadvantaged against stride competitors by the additional weight of a side-saddle. In the days when 'Ladies' Race' at point to points meant side-saddle, some serious women jockeys had special light-weight racing side-saddles made, but these are few and far between.

The difference between a stride racing saddle and the average side-saddle is in the region of 10 lbs (5 kilos).

Incidentally, old photographs of ladies competing over fences side-saddle show that many of them dispensed with the balance strap to allow the back of the saddle to rise.

## *Equitation*

In equitation classes, it is you as a rider who is being judged, but this does not mean that you can ignore your horse's performance. You cannot look your best, nor will you be considered to do your best, on an inadequately schooled horse. Some judges will not penalise you if you cope well with a buck or shy, but most will consider that you should have prevented it happening, and such displays of naughtiness will inevitably mar your performance.

Do not be tempted to think that anything less than immaculate turn-out and performance will do. Side-saddle riders take these classes extremely seriously and at the higher levels there are many who can hardly be faulted in any way. Study the rule books for requirements in each class, ensure your turn-out is absolutely as the rules say in all details, and practise your individual show until it, too, is as close to perfection as you can get it. Incidentally, make sure it is the latest rule book, as requirements can change from year to year.

## *Other Events*

Both the SSA and ISSO have special side-saddle shows with a full range of classes to be ridden side-saddle. They also stage special events, such as dressage to music or cross-country events. Some area shows have special events for novice riders which do not require you to wear a habit, and where the atmosphere is very relaxed. Typical classes at such shows include 'Handy Horse' and a variation of the old hack (Park Horse) class called The Champagne Cup. This involves the rider in performing a range of movements such as a figure of eight at the canter while carrying what was originally a glass of champagne but is now a plastic cup of water. The winner is the rider who keeps the most water in the cup.

To sum up, there are plenty of special side-saddle classes, and no bar to riding side in most other classes. If in doubt, check the relevant rule book, ask the show secretary, or go along to a similar event and see what other people do.